Chicken and Noodle Games

141 Fun Activities With Innovative Equipment

John Byl, PhD
Redeemer University College

Herwig Baldauf
Vice President of CIRA Ontario

Pat Doyle
Past President of CIRA Ontario

Andy Raithby, MA
Lisgar Middle School

Human Kinetics

Library of Congress Cataloging-in-Publication Data

Chicken and noodle games : 141 fun activities with innovative equipment / John Byl . . . [et al.]
    p. cm.
  ISBN-13: 978-0-7360-6392-0 (soft cover)
  ISBN-10: 0-7360-6392-7 (soft cover)
  1. Games. I. Byl, John.
  GV1201.C525 2007
  793--dc22

                                  2006037973

ISBN-10: 0-7360-6392-7
ISBN-13: 978-0-7360-6392-0

The Web addresses cited in this text were current as of January 2007, unless otherwise noted.

Acquisitions Editor: Gayle Kassing, PhD; **Developmental Editor:** Amy Stahl; **Assistant Editors:** Bethany J. Bentley and Carla Zych; **Copyeditor:** Annette Pierce; **Proofreader:** Red Inc.; **Permission Manager:** Dalene Reeder; **Graphic Designer:** Fred Starbird; **Graphic Artist:** Yvonne Griffith; **Photo Manager:** Neil Bernstein; **Cover Designer:** Keith Blomberg; **Photographer (cover):** © John Byl; **Photographer (interior):** Neil Bernstein, unless otherwise noted. **Art Manager:** Kelly Hendren; **Illustrator:** Keri Evans; **Printer:** Versa Press

Printed in the United States of America   10 9 8 7

The paper in this book is certified under a sustainable forestry program.

Human Kinetics
Web site: www.HumanKinetics.com

United States: Human Kinetics
P.O. Box 5076
Champaign, IL 61825-5076
800-747-4457
e-mail: humank@hkusa.com

Canada: Human Kinetics
475 Devonshire Road, Unit 100
Windsor, ON N8Y 2L5
800-465-7301 (in Canada only)
e-mail: info@hkcanada.com

Europe: Human Kinetics
107 Bradford Road
Stanningley
Leeds LS28 6AT, United Kingdom
+44 (0)113 255 5665
e-mail: hk@hkeurope.com

Australia: Human Kinetics
57A Price Avenue
Lower Mitcham, South Australia 5062
08 8372 0999
e-mail: info@hkaustralia.com

New Zealand: Human Kinetics
P.O. Box 80
Torrens Park, South Australia 5062
0800 222 062
e-mail: info@hknewzealand.com

Contents

Game Finder

Game	Page number	Chapter	Equipment	Number of players	Cost
Ab Noodle	30	2	1 medium or large noodle per team	Teams of 3 or 4 players	Minimal
Active Push 'Em Back	242	7	None	Any number of pairs	None
Activity Balloon Smash	161	4	• 1 inflated balloon per player • String	Any number of players	Minimal
Alphabet Backboard Ball	133	4	• 6-8 Gator balls • 2 alphabet puzzles	2 teams of 4-8 players	Minimal
Ambulance Relay	94	3	• 10-30 balls per team • 1 gym mat per team	Teams of 2-4 players	Moderate
Animal Keeper	122	4	1 stuffed animal per two teams	Teams of 3-6 players	Minimal
Architect	208	6	30 wood blocks of various shapes and sizes per team	Teams of 3-5 players	Minimal
Asteroids	128	4	2 sponge pieces per player	Any number of players	Minimal
Ball Scrabble	86	3	• 100 balls with letters on them • Music and music player (optional)	Teams of 4-6 players	Minimal
Balloon Fitness	160	4	• 1 inflated, labeled balloon per player • CD player • Upbeat music	Any number of players	Minimal
Balloon Keep-Ups	157	4	1 inflated balloon per group	Groups of 4-6 players	Minimal

Game	Page number	Chapter	Equipment	Number of players	Cost
Balloon Tennis	162	4	• 1 inflated balloon per group • 2 pylons per group • String • Tape	Groups of 2 or 4 players	Minimal
Battleship	72	2	• 9 medium noodles • 3 hoops or mats	Groups of 10-30 players	Minimal
Beam Balance Challenge	205	6	• Various lengths of 2 × 4s (40 × 90 mm) and other planks • Chairs (optional)	Any number of players	Minimal
Beat the Leader	81	3	• 50 tennis balls for a small group; 100 tennis balls for a large group • 1 large plastic container	Any number of players	Minimal
Beat the Wall	32	2	• 1 large noodle per player • 4 or 5 balloons per game	2 teams of 5-20 players	Minimal
Body-Part Balloon Tag	159	4	1 inflated balloon per pair	Any number of pairs	Minimal
Bodyguard Tag	180	5	None	Groups of 4-6 players	None
Bog Walk	110	4	• 36 interlocking foam squares • 1 piece of paper and 1 pencil per group	Groups of 8-12 players	Minimal
Bracelet Ball	118	4	• 2 or 3 bracelets per player • Sport-specific equipment	The number of players appropriate for the sport	Minimal
Bracelet Tag	120	4	3 bracelets per player	Any number of players	Minimal

Game	Page number	Chapter	Equipment	Number of players	Cost
Bridge Tag	182	5	None	Any number of players	None
Broken Eggs	11	1	• 1 beanbag per player • 1 rubber chicken per 8 players • 1 or more noodles	Any number of players	Moderate
Bucketball	209	6	• 2 bins or buckets • 1 basketball or Gator ball	2 teams of 5-7 players	Minimal
Careful, Minefield	204	6	• 1 rope 6-11 yards (6-11 m) long • 1 Frisbee per team • Several gymnastics mats	Groups of 4-6 players	Moderate
Carpet Shoe Sports	197	6	• 2 pieces of carpet per player • Sport-specific equipment	Teams of 5-8 players	Minimal
Catch 'Em All	90	3	• 50 tennis balls • 1 towel, blanket, or tarp per group	Groups of 2-8 players	Minimal
Catch, Throw, and Sit	10	1	1 rubber chicken per team	Teams of 3-6 players	Minimal
Chicken 500	18	1	1 fewer rubber chickens than there are players	Groups of 5-9 players	Minimal
Chicken Catching	9	1	• 1 rubber chicken per team • 1 farmer hat per team	At least 4 teams of 4-8 players	Minimal
Chicken Coops	13	1	• 1 scooter per player • 2 or more rubber chickens	2 teams of 8-12 players	Expensive

Game	Page number	Chapter	Equipment	Number of players	Cost
Chicken Juggling	15	1	2 or more rubber chickens per group	Groups of 5-6 players	Moderate
Chicken Kicking	6	1	• 6 rubber chickens • 6 ropes • Basketball hoops or soccer goals • Safety mats	Approximately 4 people per chicken	Minimal
Chicken Tag	20	1	• 1 rubber chicken per 8 players • 1 beanbag per each remaining player	Any number	Minimal
Chivalry Competition	199	6	1 carpet piece per player	Any number of pairs	Minimal
Clean Your Room	102	3	• At least 50 numbered tennis balls • A wall	2 teams of any number of players	Minimal
Clear the Chicken Coop	17	1	• At least 1 rubber chicken and beanbag per player • A badminton or volleyball court and net	2 teams of 5-12 players	Moderate
Crazy Hot Potato	141	4	• 1 wacky ball for each group • Music player • Fast-paced music	Groups of 10 players	Minimal
Deep Freeze	68	2	1 large noodle per Deep Freeze	Any number of players	Minimal
Dogcatcher	127	4	• 6-8 hoops • 2-4 pool noodles • CD player • Recording of "Who Let the Dogs Out?"	10-30 players	Minimal
Dragon Tail	144	4	1 scarf per team	Any number of players on 4-6 teams	Minimal

Game	Page number	Chapter	Equipment	Number of players	Cost
Dunk It	92	3	• 2 containers • 50 numbered balls • 2 pylons	Teams of 3-5 players	Minimal
Elbow Tag	183	5	None	Any number of players	None
Everyone It	164	4	2 clothespins per player	Any number of players	Minimal
Evolution	230	7	None	10-50 players	None
Feet-Off-the-Ground Tag	174	5	None	Any number of players	None
Fitness Frolics	112	4	• 12 interlocking foam squares • 1 marker	Teams of 4-6 players	Minimal
Follow the Leader	44	2	1 large noodle per player	Any number of players	Minimal
Four-Corner Soccer	80	3	• 50 or more tennis balls • 4 benches or floor hockey nets • 4 sets of pinnies	4 teams of 5-15 players	Moderate
Frisbee Golf	168	4	1 Frisbee per player	Up to 72 players	Minimal
Froggy Fall Over	203	6	1 soft rope per pair of players	Any number of pairs	Minimal
Garbage Can Target Toss	213	6	• 1 trash can per team • 6-10 pieces of small, tossable equipment	Teams of 3 or 4 players	Minimal
Gator Tag	190	5	• 3-6 Gator balls • 15-30 pinnies	Groups of 15-30 players	Minimal
Gauntlet	37	2	1 large or medium noodle per person on 1 team	2 teams of 5-25 players	Minimal
Go Tag	186	5	None	Groups of 10-30 players	None

Game	Page number	Chapter	Equipment	Number of players	Cost
Group Juggling	89	3	1 ball per player	Groups of 3-7 players	Minimal
Guard the Belly Button	167	4	• 3 clothespins per group • 1 pool noodle per group • 1 blindfold per group	Groups of 4-7 players	Minimal
Ha Ha	225	7	None	Any number of pairs	None
Hail, Your Highness	78	3	• 75 tennis balls per team • 1 gymnastics mat per team	Teams of 5-15 players	Moderate
Hot Dog Tag	64	2	• 1-3 large noodles • Small noodles (optional)	Any number	Minimal
Ice Cream Topple	153	4	• 15 pylons • 15 small Wiffle or tennis balls • 15 Gator balls	20-40 players	Minimal
In and Out	139	4	• 1 nylon stocking • 1 rubber ball	10-20 players	Minimal
Indoor Game Boards	198	6	• Enough carpet squares for the game chosen (9, 42, or 64) • Up to 42 pinnies or pieces of construction paper in two different colors • 24 beanbags in two different colors	2 players per game, but more if players become game pieces	Minimal
Keep It Rolling	219	6	• 1 tarp • 1 Gator ball or other soft ball per group	Groups of 4-10 players	Minimal

Game	Page number	Chapter	Equipment	Number of players	Cost
Kick-It Fence	84	3	• 50-100 tennis balls • 4 pylons	Two teams of 6-21 players	Minimal
Knights of the Round Table	65	2	• 1 or 2 medium noodles per game • 1 hula hoop, carpet square, or base per player in the circle • 1 chair	8-12 players per game	Minimal
Knotle	60	2	1 large noodle per player	A large group of players	Minimal
Letter Tag	131	4	• 1 alphabet foam puzzle • 1 activity chart	Any number of players	Minimal
Load 'Em Up	96	3	• 15-20 tennis balls per team • 1 bucket per team	Teams of 4-6 players	Minimal
Macarena Tag	188	5	• "Macarena" CD • CD player • 2 or 3 pinnies	Any number of players	Minimal
Mad Scramble Toss	82	3	50 tennis balls numbered 1-50	Up to 50 players; more if you have more numbered balls	Minimal
Man From Mars	70	2	1 large noodle per Martian	A large group of players	Minimal
Meatball in the Middle	50	2	• 8 noodles (2 small, 2 medium, 2 large, and 2 extra-large) per team • 1 Gator ball or balloon per team	Teams of 2, 4, or 6 players	Minimal

Game	Page number	Chapter	Equipment	Number of players	Cost
Mechanical Tag	215	6	• 4 bolts per 20 players • 1 nut per player • 1 pinny per 20 players	At least 20 players	Minimal
Mosquito	33	2	• 2 clothespins per player • 1 blindfold per team • 1 large noodle per team	Teams of 3-6 players	Minimal
Movement Memory	211	6	• 20 small or large trash cans • 10 pairs of matching equipment	2 teams of 3-5 players	Moderate
Moving Seats	116	4	• 1 chair per player • 1 or 2 decks of cards	At least 10 players	Minimal
Musical Chickens	3	1	• At least 1 rubber chicken per group • Music CD • CD player	Groups of 5 or 6	Minimal
Needle in the Haystack	148	4	• 3 numbered Popsicle sticks per player • 1 container	Teams of 3 players	Minimal
No-Hands Chicken	16	1	1 rubber chicken per player	Any number of players	Moderate
No Noodles in My Backyard	63	2	1 small or medium noodle per player	2 teams	Minimal
Noodle Arms	28	2	1 noodle per pair of players	Any number of pairs	Minimal
Noodle Balance	46	2	1 medium or large noodle per pair	Any number of pairs	Minimal
Noodle Head	58	2	10 small or medium noodles per team	Teams of 3-4 players	Minimal

Game	Page number	Chapter	Equipment	Number of players	Cost
Noodle Roll	42	2	At least 10 large noodles per team	Teams of about 5 players	Minimal
Noodle Target	56	2	• 1 large noodle per pair • 1 hula hoop per pair	Any number of pairs	Minimal
Noodle Waddle Relay	40	2	• 1 large or extra-large noodle per team • 1 pylon per team	Equal teams of 3 to 6 players	Minimal
Ocean Hazards	221	6	1 large blue tarp	8-15 players	Minimal
One-Down Football	235	7	1 football	Two teams of 5-7 players	Minimal
Pass the Chicken	4	1	1 rubber chicken per group	Groups of 5 or 6 players	Minimal
Pass the Pasta	62	2	1 large or extra-large noodle per team	Teams of 4-8 players	Minimal
Pennies	241	7	200 pennies	Any number of players	Minimal
Pinball	48	2	• 1 large noodle per player • At least 1 large ball per group	Groups of 5-12 players	Minimal
Pinoodle	52	2	• 1 noodle per player • 2 medium noodles • 1-5 small balls	2 teams of 5-15 players	Minimal
Pro Star Plumbers	192	6	1 toilet plunger per player	Groups of 5-10 players	Minimal
Pylon Knock-Off	155	4	• 2 benches • 12 pylons • 6 or 8 Gator balls	2 teams of 5-15 players	Minimal
Quick-Draw Four Square	226	7	None	Groups of 4-7 players	None

Game	Page number	Chapter	Equipment	Number of players	Cost
Race to Five	240	7	None	Groups of approximately 5 players	None
Racecar Tag	176	5	None	Any number of players	None
Red Stop–Green Go Tag	178	5	• 5 red pinnies • 5 green pinnies	Any number of players	Minimal
Reentry Tag	233	7	None	Any number of players	None
Rock, Paper, Scissors Mad Scramble	135	4	5-10 foam alphabet puzzles	Any number of players	Minimal
Samurai	39	2	1 large noodle	Groups of 10-15 players	Minimal
Scarf Tag	146	4	1 scarf per player	Any number of players	Minimal
Scooter Hockey	27	2	• 1 large noodle per player • 1 scooter per player • 3-6 Wiffle balls per game	2 teams of 5-12 players	Expensive
Second-Chance Tag	234	7	None	Any number of players	None
Shapes in the Dark	200	6	• 1 long rope per team • 1 blindfold per player	Teams of 3-9 players	Minimal
Shuttle Run	100	3	• 3 tennis balls per team • 3 hula hoops per team	Teams of 3 or 4 players	Minimal
Sitting Duck	98	3	• Pinnies for 2-4 teams • 1 numbered ball per player	Any number of players	Minimal

Game	Page number	Chapter	Equipment	Number of players	Cost
Slalom Run	194	6	• 2 scooters per team • 2 toilet plungers per team • 2 pylons per team	Teams of 3 or 4 players	Moderate
Snake Pit	125	4	• 5 hoops • Upbeat music • Music player	10-30 players	Minimal
Sockey	107	3	• Two hockey nets • One tennis ball	Two teams of 4-7 players	Minimal
Sponge Ball	130	4	1 sponge per player	Any number of players	Minimal
Sporting Chickens	7	1	• 1 rubber chicken per game • Other sport-specific equipment as needed	Teams of 4-12	Minimal
Square Tag	115	4	1 interlocking foam square per 5 players	5-55 players	Minimal
Stack 'Em Up	34	2	• 15-20 small and medium noodles per team • 2 large noodles per team	Groups of 3 or 4 players	Minimal
Stand Alone	236	7	1 chair per player (minus 1 for the person standing in the middle)	Groups of 7, 9, or 11 players	Minimal
Stealing the Jewels	76	3	• 2 hula hoops • 25 tennis balls per team	Two teams of 5-12 players	Minimal
Stepping-Stones	114	4	1 interlocking foam square per player	Teams of 4-6 players	Minimal
Switch-er-roo!	207	6	2 2 × 4s (40 × 90 mm) per team	Groups of 5-10 players	Minimal

Game	Page number	Chapter	Equipment	Number of players	Cost
Tank-Up Relay	196	6	• 2 scooters per team • 3 toilet plungers per team • 9 pieces of plastic pipe per team	Teams of 3 or 4 players	Minimal
Team Baseball	228	7	4 pylons for bases	2 teams of 6-12 players	Minimal
Team Chickenastics	21	1	• Rubber chickens • Gymnastics equipment, including mats • Recorded music • Music player	Groups of 2-6 players	Expensive
Ten Up	36	2	4-6 large noodles per group	Groups of 4-7 players	Minimal
Tennis Ball Relay	99	3	50-100 numbered tennis balls	Teams of 3-5 players	Minimal
Three-Stick Tag	150	4	• 3 Popsicle sticks per player • Containers	Any number of players	Minimal
Toilet Tag	184	5	3 or 4 new toilet plungers or brushes	Any number of players	Minimal
Tolkien Tag	217	6	• 18 gold-colored nuts • 3 hula hoops • 1 yellow pinny • 3 green pinnies • Tape	10-30 players	Minimal
Toss-and-Run Tag	104	3	• 50 numbered tennis balls • Recorded music • Music player	Any number of players	Minimal
Towel Baseball	142	4	• 1 towel for every 2 players • 1 ball or stuffed animal • 4 bases for the ball diamond	2 teams of 10-16 players	Minimal

Game	Page number	Chapter	Equipment	Number of players	Cost
Tower Building	166	4	50 clothespins per team	Teams of 4-6 players	Minimal
Train	238	7	None	Any number of players	None
Triangle Tag	66	2	1 large noodle per player	Groups of 4 players	Minimal
Ultimate	170	4	1 Frisbee	2 teams of 7 players	Minimal
Up and Down	151	4	20-30 minipylons	20-40 players	Minimal
Versus the Leader	232	7	None	A large group of players	None
Wacky Ball	137	4	• At least 10 rubber wacky balls • Colored pinnies • 4-6 basketball hoops	2, 4, or 6 teams of 4-8 players each	Minimal
Waddle-Walk Chin-Duck	214	6	• 2 small trash cans per team • 1 table tennis or Gator ball per team	Teams of 3 or 4 players	Minimal
World Cup	54	2	• 1 large noodle per player • 1 large ball per team	Teams of 8-15 players	Minimal
Woven-Together Web	202	6	1 ball of string	Groups of 10-15 players	Minimal
Zipper	25	2	1 large noodle per player	Groups of 8-12 or one large group	Minimal

Preface

Promoting fun and active participation for all is a worthy objective. One of the best ways to accomplish this goal is to involve players in games that do not use traditional equipment. By using unusual equipment, such as rubber chickens, pool noodles, and lots of tennis balls, sponges, and bolts, participants will find themselves on equal footing in terms of skill level. This encourages everyone to participate with intensity and to have fun.

The first goal of *Chicken and Noodle Games* is to encourage all players to have fun. Everyone remembers how rewarding moments of outrageous fun and laughter, when lost in a crazy game, can be. These moments of joviality lessen anxiety and the inclination toward depression and enhance feelings of well-being. This joy is a gift we offer to participants of fun and active games.

The second goal of this book is to increase physical activity. Active lifestyles help all people optimize their health and enjoyment of life. On the flip side are the statistics on growing obesity and the increasing amount of time people spend sedentary in front of television and computer screens. The push toward "back to basics" education has reduced student activity even more. Ironically, too much sitting around numbs the mind, making it all the more important to encourage everybody to move and increase their brain activity! Fun and active games are part of the solution for combating the ill effects of inactivity.

Approximately 90 percent of children participate in physical education classes; it is the 10 percent who do not want to be active and are least likely to participate that need attention. Games are important to everyone. Games that require little organization provide wonderful opportunities to teach inclusively (to include everyone). These games can enhance perceptual motor development; assist with focus, attention span, concentration, and perseverance; help release tension and excessive energy; assist with personal self-control; develop the thinking process; encourage social growth; and develop physical fitness and physical abilities.

Using nontraditional equipment benefits inclusive education in two ways:

1. In most cases, none of the players have had experience with the equipment; therefore, no one has an advantage or disadvantage.

2. The equipment is inexpensive and allows a game leader to provide a diverse selection of games for very little cost.

Chicken and Noodle Games was written by educators from grade schools, high schools, and postsecondary institutions who are concerned about the health of the students in their schools. These educators have experienced success with enjoyable and active games for all players and want to share them with you. They have selected their favorite games and included them here. The games are divided into seven chapters: games using rubber chickens, foam pool noodles, and tennis balls; games of tag and rock, paper, scissors; and games with equipment bought at dollar stores and hardware stores.

We have presented each game in a way that gives you a quick idea of how it works: We name the game and state the objective for you and the players to focus on while playing. We also include the number of players, type of equipment, and setup required for each game in easy-to-read bulleted lists. The instructions take you sequentially through the rules of the game you will explain to the players. We also provide variations for many of the games. We developed many of these variations while teaching and playing the games, so look for opportunities to add variations that are suitable for your situation. And encourage your players to create variations.

We did not specify appropriate ages for the games because most of these games can be enjoyed by people of all ages. However, you may need to add a variation or extra challenge to a simple game to make it work for people with greater abilities. Think of a game like duck, duck, goose, often played in kindergarten. What happens if you play this game with everyone standing and dribbling basketballs while a couple of players go around the circle? Or what happens if you number players one through three, and while a duck and goose run around, all the number ones switch places? And all of this is done while dribbling basketballs? By thinking creatively, you can adapt any of these games to grab the interest of people of any age.

Chicken and Noodle Games helps you make a positive difference in the lives of the participants in your class or program. Your efforts, with the help of this resource, will help the players move through enjoyable games using innovative equipment. Integrating the games in this book into your activities allows you to present and promote the benefits of activity and fun to the kids you lead. Now, let's play!

Acknowledgments

CIRA Ontario is an organization whose mission is to encourage fun, active participation for all. One way we try to fulfill this mission is to help teachers teach children innovative, fun, and active games. As we began to do so, teachers and children began sharing their own games and making variations to the games we played with them. The ball kept rolling, and rolling, and rolling. One major outcome of the process is the publication of this book. To those involved with CIRA Ontario, thanks!

We want to thank the following creative people who helped us in specific ways in our game-making journey: Keith DeCoste, Rob Dyment, Judith Farris, Fanitsa Housdon, and Myra Stephen.

CAHPERD contributed to the chapter on chicken games. In particular we express our appreciation for the supportive work of Andrea Grantham and Angele Beausejour.

To all the wonderful folks at Human Kinetics, thank you for seeing our vision, trusting in our judgment, supporting us in our mission, and helping to get these games into the hands of leaders.

Finally, the bottom line is always the kids. We want to thank the kids for whom we create these games, and who in turn teach us so much.

Thank you all!

Chapter 1

© Human Kinetics

Rubber Chicken Games

Rubber chickens are a delightful equalizer when used in almost any game. Take a game like basketball or football. Use the existing rules, except replace the ball with a rubber chicken—although being able to dribble a rubber chicken is unlikely—and then watch the fun as the best athlete and the most uncoordinated player are suddenly at the same level, both delighting in the craziness of the game. Change the name of the end zone in football to a chicken coop and measure how many times a team successfully brings a chicken into the coop. A *fowl shot* in basketball takes on a whole new meaning.

Rubber chickens in a variety of sizes are available from most sporting goods providers and are also available in most discount stores. If you do not have enough rubber chickens, then rubber bass, stuffed animals, or beanbags also work. Remove the stereotypical expectations associated with certain pieces of equipment and add joy and inclusiveness by using rubber chickens.

Musical Chickens

Objectives

- To avoid being the last person to throw or catch a chicken when the music stops
- To learn to catch and throw

Players

Five or six players per group

Equipment

- One to three chickens per group
- Recorded music (country-type music if possible)
- CD player

Setup

The players sit (or stand so that people in wheelchairs can participate) in small circles of five or six. Each group gets a chicken. A CD player and CD are close by.

Instructions

1. While the music is playing, players pass the chicken to any other player in their circle. They can also toss them across the circle.
2. When the music stops, the player with the chicken shouts out a letter. The first time she gets the chicken, she yells C; the second time H, the third time I, and so on until she spells *chicken*.
3. When a player spells chicken, he stands up and is temporarily excluded from that circle's game. However, as soon as a player from another circle spells chicken, the two excluded players trade places and start over.

Tips and Variations

- For even more fun, add lots of chickens to the game.
- Spell different words, such as *egg, coop, farmer,* or *rooster*.
- Keep the same groups, but as soon as someone finishes the word, the whole group starts again with C.

Adapted, by permission, from *Zany activities with a rubber chicken.* (1995) Ottawa; Canadian Intramural Recreation Association. Copyright by Canadian Association for Health, Physical Education, Recreation and Dance (CAHPERD), www.cahperd.ca.

Pass the Chicken

Objectives

- To quickly pass the chicken from one player to another through the entire team
- To develop problem-solving skills and to work as a team

Players

Five or six players per group

Equipment

One chicken per group

Setup

Each group stands in a line. Place a chicken on the floor beside the first person in line.

Instructions

Players can play several different relay games with rubber chickens. For more ideas, see the Tips and Variations section of this game.

1. Divide the group into equal numbers of players; five or six is ideal.
2. On the leader's signal to begin, the first player picks up the chicken between his knees without using his hands.
3. He then passes the chicken to the next player in line without using his hands, who receives the chicken between her knees. That player spins and passes the chicken to the next player.
4. The first team to finish wins.

Tips and Variations

- If it is too difficult for the first people in line to pick up the chicken without using their hands, have them pick up the chicken and place it between their knees.
- Give each group several chickens to pass.
- Players lie on their backs in their relay lines. The first person picks up the chicken between her feet, lifts her legs, and rolls back, putting her feet over her head. She passes the chicken to the feet

of the person behind her. She can also twist around and pass the chicken to the feet of the next person. Repeat the passes until the chicken reaches the end of the line.

© Andy Raithby

Chicken Kicking

Objective

To kick a chicken hanging from a rope, eventually progressing to the highest chicken

Players

Approximately four players per chicken

Equipment

- Six chickens and ropes
- Soccer goals or basketball hoops to hang the chickens from
- A gymnastics mat to put under each chicken

Setup

Hang chickens by their necks at various heights around the room. The lowest chicken should be at a height that everyone can successfully kick; the highest chicken should be just out of the reach of the person with the highest jumping ability. Students distribute themselves around the room, lining up next to the chicken hung at the height they want to start with.

Instructions

1. Players choose which chicken to start with.
2. Players stand on one foot, jump and kick the chicken with their jumping foot (the foot they had been standing on), and then land on the same foot.
3. If players successfully kick the chicken, they move to the next-higher chicken. If players are unsuccessful, they move to the next-lower chicken.

Tips and Variations

- Try the same challenge, but have players stand with both feet on the ground and kick the chicken with both feet.
- Try the same challenge, but have players put one hand and one foot on the ground. Players attempt to kick the chicken with the foot that was on the ground while keeping one hand on the ground.
- For safety reasons, place a gymnastics mat under each chicken for players to jump on.

Sporting Chickens

Objective

To create equity among players by replacing traditional sports equipment with rubber chickens

Players

The minimum number of players required to play the sport

Equipment

- One rubber chicken per game (In some sports, more chickens increase the fun and mayhem.)
- Other sport-specific equipment as needed

Setup

Set up the playing area as you would for any game you normally play, but use a rubber chicken instead of the ball, puck, or Frisbee.

Instructions

1. For football, play by the regular rules. However, players arae not likely to kick conversions and field goals, and instead of awarding points for touchdowns, count how many times the players bring a chicken into the chicken coop (end zone).

2. For basketball, play by the regular rules, with the exception of dribbling (players can only advance the chicken by passing it). And of course, players will take fowl shots! Add scooters for players to sit on and a couple more chickens, and the game becomes even more fun.

3. For rugby, play by the regular rules, except players punt instead of placekick.

4. For floor hockey, play by the regular rules. To slow the game and make it more physically demanding, players put a small piece of carpet under each foot and shuffle around the room.

5. For Frisbee golf, toss a rubber chicken instead of a Frisbee and count how many throws it takes to reach the target.

6. For horseshoes, play by the regular rules. A ringer is any rubber chicken that is partially draped around the post.

7. For the game of ultimate (also known as Ultimate Frisbee), replace the Frisbee with a rubber chicken, and play by the regular rules.

Tips and Variations

- Have fun with the names by changing terms such as *goals* to *coops, referees* to *farmers, teams* to *herds,* and *complainers* to *cacklers.*
- Smaller teams allow more participants to be actively involved. For football, create teams of four or five; for basketball, make teams of five or more and use extra chickens.

Chicken Catching

Objectives

- To steal a chicken from a farmer without being touched
- To foster teamwork and develop team-building skills

Players

At least four teams of four to eight players each

Equipment

- One rubber chicken per team
- One farmer hat or other means of identifying the farmer per team

Setup

Each team places its rubber chicken in its designated area at least six paces from walls or boundaries, indoors or outside. Each team chooses a farmer, who can touch other players, to guard its chicken.

Instructions

1. Players try to steal another team's chicken without being touched by a farmer.
2. If a player steals a chicken, the game stops, the stealing team gets a point, and the chicken is returned to the farmer.
3. If a player is tagged by a farmer, she must leave the farm and go to a designated spot in the middle of the playing area and pull 25 giant weeds. Players pull a weed by placing their hands on the ground, then reaching to the sky. Once a player has completed the weed-pulling job, she can resume catching chickens.

Tips and Variations

Play the game with fewer than or more than four teams, and allow each farm to have more than one farmer.

Catch, Throw, and Sit

Objectives

- To be the first team seated after each member has caught the chicken
- To develop catching and throwing skills

Players

Teams of three to six players

Equipment

One rubber chicken per team

Setup

Each team stands in a circle, 10 paces from its farmer, who is standing in the middle of the group.

Instructions

1. On the signal to begin, the farmer throws the chicken to the first player. The player catches it, throws it back, and sits down.
2. The farmer repeats this procedure around the circle. If a player or the farmer fails to catch the chicken, that person must recover it and return to position before throwing it.
3. The first team with all its players seated is the winner.

Tips and Variations

- Using two rubber chickens, the farmer throws the first chicken to the first player, the second chicken to the second player, the first chicken to the third player, and so on.
- To keep the players active when they are waiting their turn, they walk around in their spot, acting like chickens.
- See how far away from their farmer players can get and still successfully catch and throw the chickens. Have them start at five paces, then each time the chicken makes it successfully around the circle, take five more steps back. If a team member drops the chicken, the entire team moves five paces closer. See which team can get the farthest away from the farmer (each team member must be successful at this distance).

Broken Eggs

Objective

To move without dropping the beanbag balanced on the head

Players

Any number of players

Equipment

- One beanbag per player
- One rubber chicken per farmer
- One pool noodle per fox

Setup

Designate one farmer and one or more foxes for every eight players. Players are scattered around the playing area, each balancing a beanbag on his head. The player designated as the fox also carries a pool noodle. Several players are designated as farmers, and each has a chicken on her head.

Instructions

1. On the signal, players move around the area at their own pace. Leaders can change the pace or action by asking the players to hop or skip or use another movement.
2. If the egg (beanbag) falls off a player's head, that player becomes a concerned chicken and squawks and walks like a chicken around the dropped egg.
3. The fox tries to tag chickens with a pool noodle. When a chicken is tagged she must bow to the fox (at which point the egg falls off her head).
4. The fox also has a beanbag on her head. If it falls, she must do 10 push-ups before resuming the chase.
5. The farmer picks up the dropped beanbag and places it on the chicken's head, and the chicken joins the other chickens and moves as they are moving.
6. If the chicken falls off the farmer's head he calls out "Sorry!" and puts the chicken on his head again and resumes saving the eggs. After a set time, stop the game and see how many cracked eggs are on the ground.

Tips and Variations

Divide the group into teams of 8 to 12 players. Each team has its own farmer who replaces eggs that fall off the heads of her flock. At certain times, the leader calls stop. Teams count how many broken eggs they have. The leader instructs the chickens to put the eggs on their heads and begin a prescribed movement again. The leader stops and starts the game several times and teams keep track of their number of broken eggs. The team with the fewest broken eggs wins.

Chicken Coops

Objectives

- To get more chickens into the coop than the opposing team does
- To develop throwing and catching skills

Players

Two teams of 8 to 12 players.

Equipment

- One scooter per player
- At least two chickens (a chicken painted red is a red hen, and a chicken painted green is Chicken Little)

Setup

Players ride scooters and begin on their own side of the gym.

Instructions

1. The leader starts the game by "chickening out" at center court—tossing the chickens up between two players.
2. Each team tries to throw the rubber chickens into a chicken coop (the circle at the top of the basketball key or a floor hockey goal), which is guarded by one or more old hens (goalies). Players may only advance the rubber chicken by passing it—no scootering with a rubber chicken.
3. Teams score five points for a red hen thrown into the coop but only one point for Chicken Little.
4. Team members play different positions:
   - The rooster of the walk can throw the chicken in any direction. A team may have only two of these players.
   - Hens can pass but cannot score.
   - Pullets can throw only toward their own coop.
   - The old hen guards the coop.
5. All players must cluck or crow when in possession of the rubber chicken. If they don't, they must pass the chicken to anyone on the other team.

6. Use a "chicken in" (throw in) to start the game after a score. The team scored on throws in the chicken.

7. To keep track of the score, teams put an egg (ball) in a garbage can each time they score a goal. The team that fills their garbage can first wins and is higher on the pecking order.

8. Naming teams adds to the fun. The following are examples: Scratchers, Layers, Roasters, Leghorns, or Rhode Island Reds.

Tips and Variations

- To make the game more interesting and active, use more rubber chickens.

- Use more or fewer players, chickens, or rules. Call "fowls," and penalize foul talk.

- Adapt the game as needed to increase cackling, which increases the hilarity of the game.

Adapted, by permission, from *Zany activities with a rubber chicken*. (1995) Ottawa; Canadian Intramural Recreation Association. Copyright by Canadian Association for Health, Physical Education, Recreation and Dance (CAHPERD), www.cahperd.ca.

Chicken Juggling

Objective

To juggle as many chickens as possible as a team

Players

Groups of five or six players

Equipment

Two to twelve rubber chickens per group

Setup

Each group stands in a circle with two rubber chickens per group.

Instructions

1. One player tosses a chicken into the air to another player.
2. The other player catches it and immediately tosses it to another player.
3. Once the group can do this without dropping the chicken, add the second chicken.
4. Challenge the group to try the activity with as many chickens as they can.

Tips and Variations

- Have the group try to pass as many chickens as possible clockwise around the circle without dropping any. Have them try it counterclockwise.
- Try this as a partner activity. How many chickens can two people keep in the air without dropping any?

Adapted, by permission, from *Zany activities with a rubber chicken.* (1995) Ottawa; Canadian Intramural Recreation Association. Copyright by Canadian Association for Health, Physical Education, Recreation and Dance (CAHPERD), www.cahperd.ca.

No-Hands Chicken

Objective

To find many different ways to throw and catch a rubber chicken

Players

Any number of players

Equipment

One rubber chicken per player

Setup

Players are in a scattered formation a few paces from each other so that they do not accidentally bump into each other.

Instructions

1. A player tosses and catches a rubber chicken without using his hands. He tosses and catches the chicken using as many different parts of the body as possible. For example, he could throw from the elbow and catch on a foot, throw from a foot and catch on a shoulder, and throw from the head and catch between the legs.

2. Ask a few players to demonstrate their most interesting throws and catches.

Tips and Variations

- Ask half the group to demonstrate the activity, and let the other half determine who came up with the most interesting and challenging way to throw and catch a chicken. Let the two halves switch roles.

- Try this as a partner activity for two or more players with two or more chickens. One player throws the rubber chicken, and another player catches it. Add music to the routine for a further challenge.

Adapted, by permission, from *Zany activities with a rubber chicken.* (1995) Ottawa; Canadian Intramural Recreation Association. Copyright by Canadian Association for Health, Physical Education, Recreation and Dance (CAHPERD), www.cahperd.ca.

Clear the Chicken Coop

Objectives

- To keep the coop free of chickens and eggs by tossing them over the net
- To practice throwing

Players

Teams of 5 to 12 players

Equipment

- At least one rubber chicken per player
- At least one egg (beanbag) per player
- A court divided by a badminton or volleyball net

Setup

Use a badminton court if you have a few players and a volleyball court if there are a lot of players. The net divides the court into two "coops." Put the rubber chickens and beanbags in each coop and assign a coop to each team.

Instructions

1. At the start signal, the farmers (players) try to clear the rubber chickens and eggs out of their coop and into the other coop by tossing the chickens and eggs over the net.
2. At the stop signal, teams count the chickens and eggs. (Chickens and eggs outside of the coops are counted against the team that threw them out. The leader may need to assign a farmer per side who counts out-of-bounds throws. They can either keep out-of-bounds items out of the game or toss them back in.) The team with the fewest chickens and eggs in its coop wins.

Tips and Variations

Chickens count as two points, and eggs count as one point.

Adapted, by permission, from *Zany activities with a rubber chicken.* (1995) Ottawa; Canadian Intramural Recreation Association. Copyright by Canadian Association for Health, Physical Education, Recreation and Dance (CAHPERD), www.cahperd.ca.

Chicken 500

Objective

To catch chickens and be the first to score 500 points

Players

Groups of five to nine players

Equipment

One fewer chicken per group than there are players

Setup

One person in the group is the thrower; the rest are chicken catchers. The farmer (thrower) stands with his back to the wall, and the rest of the players stand in a scattered formation several paces in front of him.

Instructions

1. The farmer turns his back to the group and tosses a rubber chicken over his head toward the group. Chicken catchers try to catch the rubber chicken.
2. After saying, "chicken, chicken, chicken, chicken," the farmer tosses another chicken.
3. Catches are scored as follows:
    - 0 points if no one catches the chicken
    - 50 points if caught by the body
    - 100 points if caught by the neck
    - 150 points if caught by the legs
    - 200 points if caught by one leg
    - −100 from last person to touch the chicken if the chicken is dropped
4. When a chicken catcher catches a chicken, she must run to the farmer and leave the chicken at his feet before returning to the group to catch another one. The chicken catchers each loudly add

Adapted, by permission, from *Zany activities with a rubber chicken*. (1995) Ottawa; Canadian Intramural Recreation Association. Copyright by Canadian Association for Health, Physical Education, Recreation and Dance (CAHPERD), www.cahperd.ca.

their own points when catching the chickens until one chicken catcher scores 500 points or more. At that point, every chicken catcher's points revert to zero and the chicken catcher who scored 500 becomes the new farmer.

Tips and Variations

Players may not push or shove other players to prevent them from retrieving a chicken.

© Andy Raithby

Chicken Tag

Objectives

- To avoid being tagged or dropping a beanbag
- To practice evasion and balance

Players

Any number of players

Equipment

- One chicken per player designated as It
- One egg (beanbag) each for the rest of the players

Setup

Designate one It per eight players. Players scatter themselves throughout a defined playing area in a gymnasium or outdoors.

Instructions

1. The player that is It carries a rubber chicken on her head to indicate that she is It. Each farmer (other players) balances an egg (beanbag) on his or her head.
2. To increase the barnyard mayhem during the game, the Its must cluck as they chase the farmers.
3. If a farmer is tagged or drops an egg, the chicken who tagged the farmer or the chicken closest to the farmer exchanges the chicken for the egg. The farmer becomes a chicken and the chicken becomes a farmer.

Tips and Variations

Play tag with the players designated as It carrying their chickens and the other players carrying their eggs.

Adapted, by permission, from *Zany activities with a rubber chicken.* (1995) Ottawa; Canadian Intramural Recreation Association. Copyright by Canadian Association for Health, Physical Education, Recreation and Dance (CAHPERD), www.cahperd.ca.

Team Chickenastics

Objective

To create a gymnastics routine in which one or more rubber chickens are a major component of the demonstration

Players

Teams of two to six players

Equipment

- One or more rubber chickens per group
- Gymnastics equipment, including mats
- Recorded music
- Music player

Setup

Equipment can be preset for all teams, or teams can arrange the equipment in a manner that suits their routine.

Instructions

1. Hold a team competition in which a group does a gymnastics routine involving rubber chickens. The routine should include balances, rolls, jumps, throws, catches, and patterns in the air.
2. Judge for choreography, team spirit, timing, nicest group, and original barnyard accomplishments.

Tips and Variations

- Emphasize safety. Be sure participants have been instructed in the safety procedures for all the moves they use.
- Use mats where necessary.

Adapted, by permission, from *Zany activities with a rubber chicken.* (1995) Ottawa; Canadian Intramural Recreation Association. Copyright by Canadian Association for Health, Physical Education, Recreation and Dance (CAHPERD), www.cahperd.ca.

Chapter 2

Oodles of Noodle Games

Pool noodles or foam pipe insulators are an exciting and creative addition to any recreation, physical education, or intramural program. Pool noodle games serve as excellent icebreakers, and they generally require little organization. They rely on the spirit of play: spontaneity and fun. Pool noodles are generally four to five inches (10-13 cm) in diameter and can easily be cut to any length. The most common size is three feet (1 m) long.

Pool noodles are well suited to all types of tag games. When players follow safety procedures for using the noodles, they are not as likely to push each other from behind and hit each other too hard, which they often do in traditional tag games. You can also use pool noodles in dance classes instead of bamboo dancing sticks. And medium-sized noodles work well with kids too bashful to hold hands.

The games in this chapter use noodles of the following sizes:

- Small: 1 to 1.5 inches (2-4 cm)
- Medium: 8 to 12 inches (20-30 cm)
- Large: 3 feet (1 m)
- Extra large: 6 feet (2 m)

Pool noodles are often available at dollar stores and usually are inexpensive. An extra-large noodle costs about two dollars.

Unless otherwise noted, the games and illustrations in this chapter are adapted, by permission, from CIRA, *Oodles of noodles.* ©2004 CIRA Ontario. The photos in this chapter are reprinted, by permission, from CIRA, *Oodles of noodles.* ©2004 CIRA Ontario.

Zipper

Objective

To build trust by having players run one at a time through two lines of players, each holding a pool noodle

Players

Large groups or teams of 8 to 12 players

Equipment

One large noodle per player

Setup

Give each player a large pool noodle. Ask the group to line up in two lines facing each other, one or two paces apart, holding their pool noodles so that they stick out from their belly. When you explain that the space between the two lines should resemble a zipper, players will quickly understand how the lines should look.

Instructions

1. Select one player who feels that she trusts the group. This player's task is to run through the zipper.

2. As she approaches the noodles, players lift the noodles, like a zipper opening. It will look a bit like a wave.

3. As more players take turns running through the zipper, players will gain confidence in the group and will increase their speed through the zipper.

Tips and Variations

- Large groups can form one large zipper; teams of 8 to 12 players can form their own. This is a great warm-up activity when done in smaller groups.

- Line-to-Line Race: Form two or more groups. Select a starting line that the zippers begin behind, standing shoulder to shoulder. The first player in each line runs through, and when these players get to the end, they stay at the end of the line. When the first players finish, the next player in each line begins. The line that crosses the finish line first wins.

- Car Wash: Use extra-large noodles. Players do not lift the noodles as other players run by, but keep them out for the runner to hit. The second players in line do not have to wait until the players before them have come to the end, but can begin after they have run through five noodles.

- Broken Zipper: Players use large noodles. When the runner goes by, players try to hit him on the back.

Scooter Hockey

Objective

To score goals against the other team, using pool noodles and Wiffle balls

Players

Two teams of 5 to 12 players

Equipment

- Three to six plastic Wiffle balls (a larger version of plastic practice golf balls)
- One large pool noodle per player
- One scooter per player

Setup

- Assign each group half of the playing area, with a goal at the back of each end. If you are playing in the gym, the goal can be the back of the basketball key (there are no goalies).
- Players begin in a scattered formation around the gym.

Instructions

1. Each player sits on a scooter and uses a pool noodle as a hockey stick. The Wiffle balls are used as pucks.
2. Begin play by tossing the Wiffle balls onto the floor.
3. Players are not allowed in the basketball key (or similar area around the goal), but they may reach into it with the noodles.
4. After a goal is scored, a defensive player can enter the crease and pass the ball to one of his players to resume play.

Tips and Variations

Remind players to keep their fingers away from the scooter wheels.

Noodle Arms

Objective

For partners to run while supporting a noodle between their hips

Players

Any number of pairs

Equipment

One noodle of any size per pair of players

Setup

- Establish a starting line and a finish line 10 to 20 paces apart.
- Give each pair one noodle.
- Standing side by side on the starting line, players put the noodle between them and hold it in place with their hips. They will move in a manner similar to a three-legged race: players are stuck together and must work as a team.
- This activity can be done as a warm-up or a race.

Instructions

1. All teams line up along the starting line. At the signal, pairs race to the finish line (or complete a certain number of laps around a course). If a team's noodle falls, that team must pick it up and go back to the beginning.
2. Players cannot touch the noodle with their hands to keep it in place.

Tips and Variations

- Hip Sports: Play any sport that requires a lot of arm use, e.g., basketball, volleyball, floor hockey. The rules stay the same, but every player must stay attached to his or her partner. If the noodle falls directly after a shot, the basket or goal does not count.
- For sports that require more use of the feet than the arms, such as in soccer, play in the same way, but the pool noodle must stay between the partners' forearms instead of hips.

Ab Noodle

Objective

To be the first team to pass a noodle from one end of the playing area to the other with their feet

Players

Any number of teams of three or four

Equipment

One medium or large noodle per team

Setup

- Give each team a pool noodle.
- Designate a starting line and finish line (from one end of the gym to the other).
- Each team forms a line perpendicular to the starting line by lying on the ground with their heads toward the starting line and knees bent. The head of the first player is on the starting line with the noodle near her head just behind the line. The head of the next player is at her feet.

Instructions

1. At the signal, the first player grabs the noodle from near her head, performs a sit-up, and puts the noodle into the hands of the next player.
2. As soon as the first player has released the noodle, she stands up and runs to the end of the line.
3. The second player does the same thing.
4. The pattern continues until the pool noodle touches the finish line.
5. The first team to get its noodle to the other side wins.

Tips and Variations

- This is a great abdominal warm-up.
- Safety tip: Players should keep their knees bent while performing the sit-up, pass the noodle gently, and keep their hands up to protect their faces while receiving the noodle.
- Reverse Ab Noodle: Play the same game in reverse, going from the finish line to the start line. The noodle begins at the feet of the first player and is passed backward over his head to the next player's feet.

Beat the Wall

Objective

To score on the opposing team's goal, using a balloon and pool noodles

Players

Two teams of 5 to 20 players

Equipment

- One large noodle for every player
- Three or four balloons per game (but have four or five on hand in case some pop)

Setup

This game is best played in a gym. Each team begins on one half of the playing area and must protect its goal: the end wall.

Instructions

1. Play begins by throwing a balloon into the air at center court. Players keep the balloon in the air with their pool noodles and cannot touch the balloon with any part of their body. If the balloon touches the floor, players continue to hit the balloon with their noodles.
2. Teams work together to move the balloon into the other team's zone. Teams score a point when the balloon hits the end wall.
3. After a goal is made, return the balloon to center court to resume play.

Tips and Variations

Safety tips: There should be no body contact between players. To prevent ankle injuries, warn players not to jump.

Mosquito

Objective

To put as many mosquitoes (clothespins) as possible on the player in the middle

Players

Teams of three to six players

Equipment

- Two clothespins per player (Color code the pins so that it is easy to count how many pins each team placed on the volunteer.)
- One blindfold per team
- One large pool noodle per team

Setup

- Explain to the players that mosquitoes like to attach themselves to people. (You could also change the name of game to leaches or to another animal that likes to attach itself to people.)
- Each team sends a volunteer to stand blindfolded in the middle of the playing area. The volunteer has a large pool noodle. The team of mosquitoes stands around the blindfolded player.

Instructions

1. Players from each team take turns approaching the players in the middle and attempting to attach clothespins to their clothing. If the blindfolded person swats a mosquito (hits a player with her noodle), the swatted player returns to his team.
2. The team that places the most mosquitoes on the players in the middle wins.

Tips and Variations

- This game is well suited for teenagers and adults.
- Mosquito—All Against One: Divide the group into teams and choose one player to stand blindfolded in the center of the playing area. On the go signal, all players try to attach their mosquitoes to the victim while he defends himself with a pool noodle.

Stack 'Em Up

Objectives

To collect as many small and medium noodles as possible and to stack them into one large tower

Players

Groups of three or four

Equipment

- Fifteen to twenty small and medium noodles per team
- Two large noodles per team

Setup

- Scatter the small and medium noodles around the playing area.
- Line up the teams along the edges of the playing area. Designate a building location for each team.

Instructions

1. Each team starts in its building space. On the *go* signal, the two retrievers run into the playing area with two large noodles. Holding onto opposite ends of the noodles, the players attempt to pick up the smaller noodles without touching them with their hands.
2. The retrievers take the noodles to the building space, and then run back out to get more noodles.
3. The builder stacks the noodles as high as possible.
4. Play continues until all the noodles are collected and stacked. Players should rotate as retrievers and builders. The team with the highest tower wins.

Tips and Variations

Add 'Em Up: Assign point values to the small and medium noodles, according to size and color (e.g., medium red noodles are worth three points, small blue noodles are worth five points, and so on). Instead of stacking the noodles, the third player on each team totals the point values.

Ten Up

Objectives

- To earn 10 points by catching noodles
- To practice catching

Players

Groups of four to seven

Equipment

Four to six large noodles per group

Setup

- This is a variation of the baseball game called 500 Up.
- Each group has its own assigned area.
- A thrower from each group stands at the front, facing the players, who are scattered around the playing area 5 to 10 paces away from the thrower.

Instructions

1. The thrower throws a noodle, and the players attempt to catch it before it hits the floor or ground. Catching a noodle in the air is worth 2 points; picking up a dropped noodle is worth 1 point.
2. When a player earns 10 points, she can become the thrower if she is able to perform the skill. If not, another player throws the noodles.
3. If two players catch or pick up a noodle at the same time, they play rock, paper, scissors to determine who gets the points (see chapter 7 for instructions for playing rock, paper, scissors). While they are playing, the thrower can throw the next noodle.
4. The person who catches the noodle returns it to the thrower.

Tips and Variations

Ten Up, Partner Up: If you have a lot of players, ask each player to find a partner. One player stands in the playing area and the other waits on the sidelines. When a player catches a noodle, he takes it to his partner and stays on the sidelines. His partner returns the noodle to the leader and takes a turn in the field.

Gauntlet

Objective

To run from one side of the playing area to the other as many times as possible

Players

Two teams of 5 to 25 players.

Equipment

One large or medium noodle per person on one team

Setup

One team stands at one end of the playing area behind the end line, and the other team spreads out on either side of the playing area along the sidelines to form the gauntlet (a volleyball court works well). Each player on the gauntlet team has one noodle.

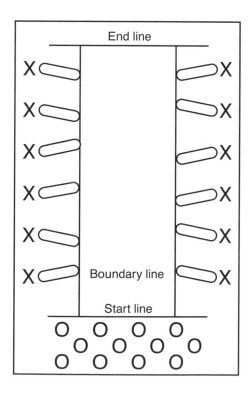

Instructions

1. When the leader says go, all the players from the first team try to run through the gauntlet without being hit by a noodle thrown from the sidelines.
2. The throwers must stay behind the sidelines when throwing.
3. Players who are hit must sit down where they were hit and can help their teammates by providing brief stationary shelters for runners to briefly hide behind.
4. The remaining players run the gauntlet again.
5. Play until everyone has been hit, and then the next team has a turn.

Tips and Variations

Gauntlet Treasure: Place items at the end of the gauntlet for players to collect and return to the other side.

Samurai

Objectives

To follow the leader and to avoid being hit by the noodle

Players

Groups of 10 to 15

Equipment

One large noodle

Setup

- All the players stand in a circle (about 10 paces across) and select one player to be the samurai (leader).
- The samurai stands in the middle of the circle with a large noodle.

Instructions

1. From the middle of the circle, the samurai waves the noodle around. She then runs to a player or group of players in the circle and swings the noodle either near their chests or near their feet.
2. Players have to duck or jump to avoid being hit. If someone does not duck or jump quickly enough, he becomes the samurai.
3. In big groups, play with more than one samurai. This means that players have to watch both samurais at the same time.

Tips and Variations

A samurai cannot swing at the same player two times in a row.

Noodle Waddle Relay

Objective

To be the fastest team to complete the relay

Players

Equal teams of three to six players

Equipment

- One large or extra-large noodle per team
- One pylon per team

Setup

- Give each team a large or extra-large noodle.
- Establish a starting line.
- Set up a pylon for each team approximately 10 paces away from the starting line.

Instructions

1. The teams line up behind the starting line. The first player on each team has a noodle between his knees. At the start signal, he waddles around the pylon and back.

2. When he returns to his team, he passes the noodle to the next player. Neither of them can touch the noodle with their hands. If they touch the noodle with their hands, the team must start again from the beginning.

3. The players continue waddling to the pylon and back and passing to the next player. The first team to finish wins.

Tips and Variations

Pick-Up Noodle Relay: When the first player is finished, the next player joins him on the noodle, and both run the next leg of the relay together. Then they pick up the next player, and so on.

Noodle Roll

Objective

To be the first team to roll a player across the finish line

Players

Teams of about five players

Equipment

At least 10 large noodles per team

Setup

- Designate a starting line and a finish line about 10 paces apart (the width of a volleyball court works well).
- Behind the starting line, one player on each team (the log) lies on her back across a bed of noodles with her head near the starting line.

Instructions

1. At the signal to start, one player begins to push the feet of the log, who remains rigid.
2. The other players on the team remove noodles from under his feet to the front, so that the log's bed of noodles never ends.
3. The first team to roll over the finish line wins.

Tips and Variations

Safety tip: The log should stay on her back with her hands behind her head to avoid contact with the ground and to protect her head and hair.

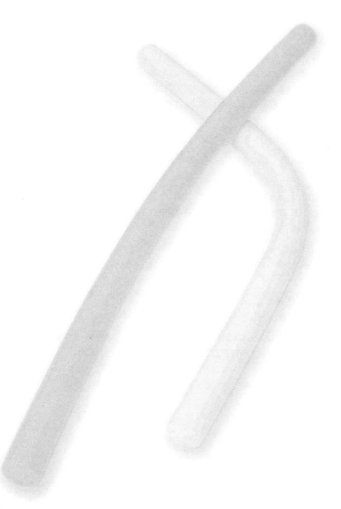

Follow the Leader

Objectives

To watch what the leader does with the noodle and to become adept at the same tricks and skills

Players

Any number of players

Equipment

One large noodle per player

Setup

Players are scattered throughout the playing area (one large noodle-length away from other players) facing the leader.

Instructions

1. The leader shows the group a variety of challenges (the more creative the better), and the group tries to copy him and to perform the challenges.

2. Possible challenges include the following:
   - Hold the noodle at one end, let go, and catch it at the other end.
   - Hold the noodle in the middle and place the other hand behind the back. Let go and try to switch hands without letting the noodle fall to the ground.
   - Balance the noodle on the hand. This can be done as a competitive elimination game, eliminating players when their noodle falls.
   - Balance the noodle on one palm, toss it in the air, and catch it on the other palm.
   - Balance the end of the noodle on the palm, toss it so that it flips in the air, and catch the other end with the palm.

Tips and Variations

- This activity gives everyone an opportunity to become familiar with the noodles and to try various activities.
- Ask the players to challenge the group with their own challenges. This provides a leadership opportunity for the players.

Noodle Balance

Objective

To pull or push an opponent off balance

Players

Any number of pairs, one player against another

Equipment

One medium or large noodle per pair

Setup

- Opponents stand next to each other facing opposite directions, with the outside of one partner's foot against the outside of the other partner's foot. Each player's feet are at least shoulder-width apart.
- The players hold opposite sides of a pool noodle.

Instructions

1. On the signal to begin, both players push and pull the pool noodle, trying to knock the other player off balance.
2. The first player to lift or move a foot loses the contest.

Tips and Variations

Players may only push or pull through the pool noodle. A player cannot make contact with the other player except through the one foot.

Pinball

Objective

To roll the ball out of the circle through someone else's legs

Players

Groups of 5 to 12 players

Equipment

- One large noodle per player
- One (or more) large ball per group

Setup

Give each player one noodle and have players stand in a circle with their backs facing in and their feet touching the feet of player beside them, shoulder-width apart.

Instructions

1. Roll a ball into the middle of the circle. If it is a large group, you can play with more than one ball.
2. Players try to roll the ball out of the circle through someone else's legs by hitting the ball with the noodle. Players also use the noodles to try to prevent the ball from rolling through their own legs and out of the circle.
3. Players may not touch the ball with their hands.

Tips and Variations

None

Meatball in the Middle

Objective

To carry a Gator ball across the gym by squeezing it between two pool noodles

Players

Teams of two, four, or six players

Equipment

- Eight noodles (two small, two medium, two large, and two extra large) per team
- One ball or balloon per team

Setup

- Designate a starting line and a finish line.
- Give each team two noodles of each size and one ball or balloon.
- Each player selects a partner, and teams line up on the starting line by twos.

Instructions

1. At the signal, the first pair on each team picks up the Gator ball with the small noodles and walks to the finish line and back. The pair holds the ball between the ends of the two noodles. Only the ends of the noodles may touch the ball. When the pair returns, they set the ball on the ground and then the next pair goes, using the same noodles.
2. When every pair has gone, the first team goes again, using the medium noodles.
3. The process continues until each pair has gone to the finish line and back, carrying the Gator ball with noodles of every size. If this challenge is too difficult with the extra-large noodles, the players can cradle the ball on top of two noodles. If players drop the ball, they return to the start line and try again with the same noodle lengths.
4. The first team to finish wins.

Tips and Variations

- To make this game less difficult, use a balloon instead of a Gator ball.
- How Many Small Noodles: Use only small noodles, increasing the number of noodles instead of the size. In this variation, the noodles are pressed together side by side, and players can only touch the outside noodles.

Pinoodle

Objective

To knock over the other team's pin

Players

Two teams of 5 to 15 players

Equipment

- One medium noodle per player
- Two medium noodles as "pins" or two plastic bowling pins
- One to five small Gator, foam, or Wiffle balls

Setup

- Divide the playing area in half and assign each team a half.
- At the back of each team's area, place one medium noodle upright on its end to serve as the pin and assign a zone around it that players cannot enter (the top of a basketball key works well). Teams select one player to be the pin protector, who guards the pin. The pin protector is the only player allowed in the zone.

Instructions

1. Teams play as they would play floor hockey, but they use several balls and use noodles instead of sticks.
2. Teams score a point each time they knock over a pin. After each point, the pin protector sets up the pin and play continues.

Tips and Variations

None

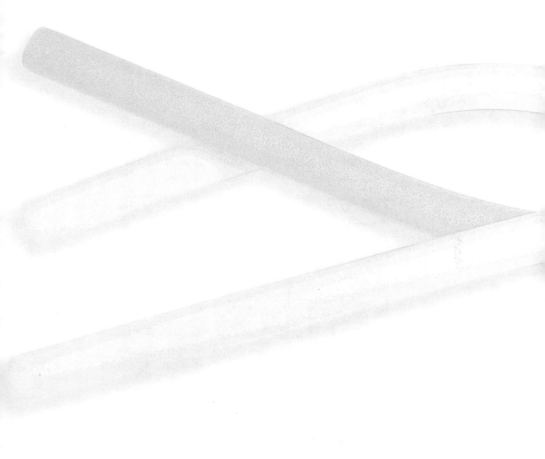

World Cup

Objectives

- To carry a ball as far as possible using pool noodles
- To develop problem-solving and team-building skills

Players

Teams of 8 to 15 players

Equipment

- One large noodle per player
- One large Gator ball or beach ball per team

Setup

- Give every player a large noodle and give every team a large ball.
- Specify a starting line and turnaround point for each team.

Instructions

1. Teams stand at the starting line and work together to lift the ball with the noodles. No one may touch the ball with the hands.
2. Once the ball is over their heads, the team must move as a group to the turnaround point and back to the starting line without dropping the ball. If the ball falls, the entire team returns to the beginning and starts over.
3. The first team to make it to the turnaround point and back wins.

Tips and Variations

Timed World Cup: Each team sees how far it can travel in a specified time. Players will learn that going quickly is not the best strategy if it results in dropped balls and starting over.

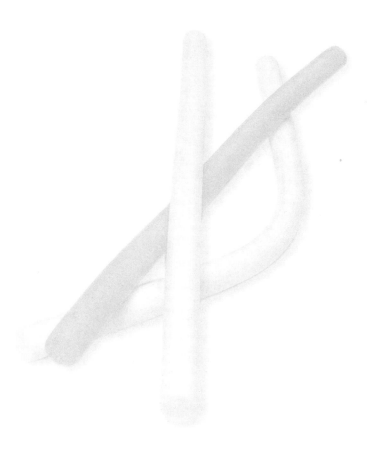

Noodle Target

Objectives

- To throw a noodle and hit a target
- To continue increasing the distance to the target

Players

Any number of pairs; for a large group or for younger children, two pairs rather than two individuals, can be partners

Equipment

- One large noodle per pair
- One hula hoop per pair

Setup

- Partners stand facing each other. They are about the length of one large noodle apart.
- One player has the hula hoop, and the other has the noodle.

Instructions

1. One player holds a hula hoop as a target for the other player. The other tries to throw the noodle through the hoop.

2. The player holding the hoop can move the hoop, but she cannot move her feet.

3. If the throw is successful, the player holding the hoop takes one big step backward, and the thrower tries again from this distance. If the throw is not successful, the hoop holder takes one step closer.

4. The pair to hit the target from the farthest distance wins.

5. Switch player roles and try again.

Tips and Variations

Human Target: Play the same way, but start the length of two large noodles apart, and instead of aiming for a hoop, players try to catch their partner's throw.

Noodle Head

Objective

To stack as many noodles as possible on a team member's head

Players

Teams of three or four players

Equipment

Ten small or medium noodles per team

Setup

- Designate a starting line and finish line.
- Assign a team leader from each team to sit cross-legged at the finish line.
- The rest of the team stands at the starting line. Beside each team is a pile or a bin of small or medium noodles.

Instructions

1. On the go signal, the first player takes a noodle, runs to the team leader, places it on his head, and runs back to the team. The leader can only touch the noodles with one hand.
2. The players proceed one at a time, stacking noodles on the head of the team leader.
3. If the stack falls, the player attempting to place the noodle picks up the fallen noodles and brings them back to the team. Another option is for the player to restack the noodles, costing the team time only.
4. Stop the game after a specified time. The team with the highest stack wins.

Tips and Variations

- Players can work in pairs and use large noodles to carry and place the smaller noodles on the head of the leader.
- Noodle-Head Relay: Play the game with no team leader. Instead, the first player places one noodle on her head and runs to the

finish line and back, passing the noodle with his hands to the next player who does the same thing. When every player has done this, the first player goes again, this time with a stack of two on her head. Continue until every player has run the relay carrying a stack of three noodles. When the noodles fall off a player's head, he must stop and put them back on his head before continuing. This game can also be played individually.

Knotle

Objectives

- To untangle a maze of players
- To learn to solve problems and develop team-building skills

Players

A large group of players

Equipment

One large noodle per player

Setup

A group of players stands in a tight circle, each holding one end of a noodle with one hand.

Instructions

1. Players extend the end of their noodle anywhere else in the circle, and another player grabs the end. Each player is now holding two different noodles and the group is entangled in a maze or knot.
2. The group must then untangle themselves, forming a new circle, without anyone letting go of the noodles at any time.

Tips and Variations

None

Pass the Pasta

Objective

To pass the noodle across the playing area as quickly as possible without dropping it

Players

Teams of four to eight players

Equipment

One large or extra-large noodle per team

Setup

Line up all teams at one end of the playing area. Designate a start and finish line.

Instructions

1. The first player in each line places the noodle between his legs and passes it to the next player. Neither player can use his or her hands.
2. The second player takes the noodle between her knees, turns to the next player, and passes it on.
3. After passing the noodle, players run to the end of the line, getting ready to pass the noodle again.
4. The first team to move the noodle across the playing area without dropping it or touching it with their hands wins.
5. If the noodle is dropped or if players touch the noodle with their hands, the whole team must move back to the beginning of the playing area and begin again.

Tips and Variations

None

No Noodles in My Backyard

Objective

To throw all the noodles onto the other team's side

Players

Two teams of any number of players

Equipment

One small or medium noodle per player

Setup

- Give each player one noodle.
- Divide the playing area in half and assign each team to a half. Players stay on their side of the playing area.

Instructions

1. At the signal to begin, players throw their noodles onto the other team's side of the playing area.
2. Players pick up noodles and throw them, trying to clean up their zone.
3. At the signal, players stop immediately.
4. Teams count the number of noodles in their zones. The team with the fewest noodles wins.

Tips and Variations

Play fast-paced music throughout the game, and stop the music to end the game.

TAG GAMES WITH POOL NOODLES

Traditional tag games are as old as games themselves. By adding noodles to tag games, players will enjoy using new equipment and will enjoy a safer and faster tag experience. Leaders must be consistent and clear in explaining acceptable rules for hitting others. A good rule is never to hit to hurt; only hit to eliminate. Another safety rule for all tag games is that players must tag only below the waist.

Hot Dog Tag

Objective

To avoid being tagged, or to tag as many other players as possible

Players

Any number of players

Equipment

- One to three large noodles
- Small colored noodles (optional)

Setup

Players scatter themselves throughout the playing area. One to three players are designated as It. Each It has a pool noodle with which to tag the other players.

Instructions

1. The Its chase the other players around the playing area and try to tag them using a pool noodle.
2. When a player is tagged, she must lie on her back on the ground and yell, "I need buns!" She cannot stand up and continue to play until two other players lie down beside her, one on each side.

Tips and Variations

- Change Its frequently.
- Add small colored noodles as "condiments." The tagged player cannot stand up until she has two buns as well as ketchup and mustard, which other players must place on top of her.

Knights of the Round Table

Objective

To stay out of the middle of the circle by either safely reaching the outside of the circle or by quickly hitting another player with a pool noodle

Players

8 to 12 players per game

Equipment

- One or two medium noodles per game
- One chair
- One hula hoop (or carpet square or base) per person in the circle

Setup

- The rest of the players take a hula hoop and create a large circle. Players sit in their hoops.
- Place the chair with one pool noodle on it in the middle of the circle and select a player to begin there.

Instructions

1. Player A in the middle of the circle takes the noodle and hits another player, player B, with it. Player A runs and puts the noodle back on the chair and then tries to quickly get to player B's hoop.
2. As soon as player B is hit, she stands up, runs to grab the noodle from the chair, and tries to hit player A before he can get to the hoop. If player B hits player A, then player B returns to her hoop, and player A goes back to the middle to try to hit another player.
3. If player B does not hit player A, or if player A gets to the hoop successfully, then player B stays in the middle and begins again.
4. Once the players get the hang of this, add another noodle to the chair and start two people in the middle.

Tips and Variations

- Moving Seats: In this variation, the players sitting in the circle can move into an empty hoop beside them. The players running back to the hoop have to escape the noodle and find the empty hoop.

Triangle Tag

Objective

To tag the player on the opposite side of the triangle

Players

Groups of four

Equipment

One large noodle per player

Setup

- Three players form a triangle by holding pool noodles between them. One of these players is designated as the target.
- One player outside of the triangle is designated as It.

Instructions

1. The It must stay outside the triangle and attempt to hit the target with her noodle.

2. The other two players try to protect the target by moving the triangle so that it is difficult for the It to hit the target.

3. Once the It hits the target or a specified time has passed, someone else has a turn outside the triangle.

Tips and Variations

- Circle Tag: In this more difficult variation, play in groups of four to six and create squares or circles. Determine who is It and who is the target and let the activity roll.

- Chain Tag: Five or six players form a chain by holding hands. The person at the front has a noodle and must try to tag the player at the back while the players keep the chain intact. Once the player in the front tags the player in back, the tagged player moves to the front and becomes the hitter.

Deep Freeze

Objectives

- To avoid being tagged by Deep Freeze
- For Deep Freeze to tag as many players as possible

Players

Any number of players

Equipment

One large noodle per Deep Freeze

Setup

- Play this game in a gym where there are a lot of lines on the floor. Basketball court lines work well.
- Select one or two players to be Deep Freeze. Give each Deep Freeze a noodle to tag other players with.

Instructions

1. Players are allowed to travel only along the lines on the floor. When a player is tagged, he must sit down on the line where he was tagged, creating an obstacle for other players. Other players may not move over or around these frozen players; however, Deep Freeze can.

2. Eventually players will become trapped between two tagged players, and tagging them becomes easier.

3. Switch the Deep Freezes often, or allow the last untagged players to become the next Deep Freeze.

Tips and Variations

Deep Freeze vs. Deep Thaw: For every Deep Freeze, assign another player to be Deep Thaw. This player uses a noodle of a different color to instantly thaw players who have been frozen.

Man From Mars

Objectives

- To run across the playing area without being tagged by the Man From Mars
- For the Man From Mars to tag players as they run toward him

Players

A large group

Equipment

One large noodle per Martian

Setup

- Assign one or two players to be Martians, give each one a pool noodle, and ask them to stand in the middle of the playing area.
- The rest of the players line up along one side of the playing area.

Instructions

1. The Martians in the middle quickly discuss what command they will give, and then shout it out: *I am the man, the man from mars, and I will chase you to the stars if* [*you are wearing blue, you have a cat, you are 10 years old, your birthday is in June,* and so on]. With younger players, the leader gives most of these commands.

2. The players who fit the command must run to the other side of the playing area without being tagged.

3. Players who are tagged are eliminated and must sit on the sidelines.

4. As more players are eliminated, add the rule that if the Martians do not tag anyone, all eliminated players can return to the game.

Tips and Variations

Safety tip: To prevent younger players from running toward each other, allow players to cross the playing area only if the Martians are facing them.

Battleship

Objectives

To safely cross the playing area

Players

Groups of 10 to 30 players

Equipment

- Nine medium noodles
- Three hoops or mats

Setup

Place three battleships (hoops or mats) across the center of the floor. Select three players to serve as sailors on the battleships and attack the remaining players. Give each sailor three noodles to use as missiles. The rest of the players line up at one end of the playing area.

Instructions

1. The leader and sailors shout "battleship!" as the signal for the players to cross the playing area, trying to avoid being hit by missiles. The sailors can swing or throw the missiles.
2. When a player is hit, she becomes a land mine and must stand in the spot where she was hit and tag players who run by her. The players she tags also become land mines. You can give these players pool noodles to make the game more challenging.
3. Sailors can retrieve their missiles after every player has reached the other side or has been tagged.
4. The game is over when all players have become land mines.

Tips and Variations

Battleship With Medics: Players decide on one medic but do not let the sailors know who she is. When she runs across and contacts land mines, the land mines become freed players again. Once the sailors determine who the medic is and contact her with a noodle, the game is over.

Game adapted from *Great Gator Games,* CIRA Ontario. 1998. Hamilton, Ontario, Canada: CIRA Ontario. Many other games from *Great Gator Games* can be used with noodles instead of Gator balls.

Chapter 3

Tennis Ball Games

We had a lot of fun creating these tennis ball games. We know you'll have even more fun playing them and developing fun variations and totally new games.

In preparation for most of these games, you'll need 50 tennis balls or more—the more the merrier. You can purchase these balls very cheaply at dollar stores or receive free discarded balls from a local tennis club. Typically, the balls do not need a lot of bounce, so any tennis balls will do. Once you have collected enough balls, letter them.

The games in this chapter are adapted, by permission, from CIRA, *50 games with 50 tennis balls*. ©2003 CIRA Ontario. The photos in this chapter are reprinted, by permission, from CIRA, *50 games with 50 tennis balls*. ©2003 CIRA Ontario.

Stealing the Jewels

Objective

To try to steal jewels (tennis balls) from the opposing team

Players

Two teams of 5 to 12 players

Equipment

- Two hula hoops
- Twenty-five tennis balls per team

Setup

- Each team gets one hula hoop and 25 tennis balls.
- Place the tennis balls inside the hula hoops, which are lying on the ground at least five paces apart from each other.
- Designate one guard on each team to stand inside the hoop to guard the jewels. The rest of the team stands around the opposing team's hoop.

Instructions

1. Players try to steal the jewels without letting the guard touch them with his hands.
2. If a player is tagged while stealing a ball, he must return it and do 25 jumping jacks where he was tagged. Afterward, he can resume his stealing ways.
3. Once a ball is stolen, it is placed in the other team's hoop.
4. After a specified time, players count how many jewels each team has. The team with the most is the winner.
5. Change the guards in subsequent games.

Tips and Variations

Blindfold the guard and give her a pool noodle. When she touches thieves with the noodle, they must freeze.

Hail, Your Highness

Objectives

- To be the first team to quickly roll a folded mat from the starting line to the finish line
- To learn teamwork

Players

Teams of 5 to 15 players

Equipment

- Seventy-five tennis balls per team
- One folded gymnastics mat per team

Setup

- Designate a starting line and finish line.
- Place the folded mats on the starting line. Each team puts their tennis balls under their mat.
- Designate one player as Your Highness. He or she lies on the mat.

Instructions

1. On the *go* signal, one player from each team pushes the mat with Your Highness on it toward the finish line while the rest of the team retrieves the balls left behind as the mat moves forward. Players place these balls under the front of the mat to allow it to continue rolling forward.

2. The team that gets Your Highness to the finish line first is the winner.

Tips and Variations

- Add people on the mat.
- Use volleyballs or basketballs instead of tennis balls.

Four-Corner Soccer

Objectives

- To allow as few goals as possible
- To practice kicking skills and teamwork

Players

Four teams of 5 to 15 players

Equipment

- Fifty or more tennis balls
- Four benches to use as goals (or four floor hockey nets)
- Four sets of pinnies

Setup

- Place a bench in each corner of the playing area to serve as a goal.
- Players scatter themselves throughout the gym. Colored pinnies help distinguish teams.

Instructions

1. Throw out all the tennis balls. Players kick the balls to try to score on any goal but their own. If a player kicks a ball through a bench, she should ensure that it stays in the goal. If the benches are laid on their side, any ball that hits the bench scores. The shooter can pick up the ball and place it behind that bench to count as a goal.
2. Players continue for a certain amount of time or until all the balls have scored. The team with the *fewest* balls behind its bench is the winner.

Tips and Variations

Ball Collector: This game is similar to Four-Corner Soccer, except that each team tries to collect (kick and score) as many balls in their goal as possible. Other teams may protect other team goals, but no goalie may use his or her hands.

Beat the Leader

Objectives

- To fill a container with tennis balls more quickly than the leader can empty it
- To develop building, throwing, catching, and teamwork skills

Players

Any number of players

Equipment

- Fifty tennis balls for a small group, 100 tennis balls for a large group
- One large plastic container

Setup

The leader stands next to the plastic container in the middle of the playing area. Place the tennis balls in the container. The players stand scattered around the container.

Instructions

1. On the *go* signal, the leader tries to empty the container by throwing out balls one by one.
2. The players try to put all the tennis balls back inside the container before the leader empties it. Players will find it helpful for some people to remain close to the container. Other players can pass balls to these people, who can place them in the container.
3. You may need to change the leader from time to time.

Tips and Variations

- Increase or decrease the number of balls.
- Add other equipment such as Gator balls, Frisbees, or beanbags.

Mad Scramble Toss

Objective

To retrieve the ball that has your number on it

Players

Up to 50 players; more if you have more numbered balls

Equipment

Tennis balls numbered 1 through 50

Setup

- Assign each player a number.
- The leader stands in the center of the playing area with a box of numbered tennis balls.
- Players are in a circle around the leader.

Instructions

1. Toss out the balls.
2. On the *go* signal, players run and retrieve their ball and return to their designated spot. The first player to succeed is the winner.

Tips and Variations

- Each time a player picks up a ball, she calls out the number.
- Players should play as a team. The team works together and is finished when everyone has found his or her ball.

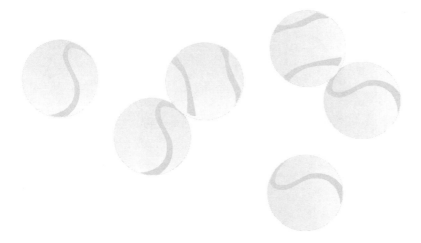

Kick-It Fence

Objectives

- To kick as many balls as possible into your opponent's goal
- To learn kicking and teamwork skills

Players

Two teams of 6 to 21 players each

Equipment

- Fifty to one hundred tennis balls
- Four pylons to designate goals (two paces apart)

Setup

- Teams form three-person fences by locking elbows or holding hands. If players are left over after forming the fences, create one or two two-person fences.
- Teams spread out on their half of the playing area.
- Goals are set up on either end of the playing area.

Instructions

1. The leader drops all the balls into the middle of the playing area and players begin to kick the balls, trying to penetrate their opponents' fence and kick balls into the goal.
2. All balls that end up in the goal score a point. If team members break apart, they must rejoin before resuming play.

Tips and Variations

None

Ball Scrabble

Objective

To create as many words as possible from the letters on the team's tennis balls

Players

Teams of 4 or 6

Equipment

- One hundred balls with letters on them
- Music and music player (optional)

Setup

- Place 50 lettered balls in the center of the playing area.
- Designate a spelling spot for each team approximately five paces away from the balls.

Instructions

1. Teams gather in their spot. On the *go* signal, players run to the center of the playing area. Each picks up one ball (or two if the groups are small) and returns to the spelling spot.
2. Once the music begins, players create as many words as they can with the letters on their balls.
3. When the music stops, groups tally the number of words they formed. The team with the most words is the winner.
4. After the words have been counted, players roll the balls back to the middle of the playing area and start a new game.

Tips and Variations

- Give different letters different point values. Players still create words but tally the points used rather than the number of words created.
- Give extra points for any word of more than three letters.

- See which team can make the longest word and score one point for each letter used.
- Players connect the words, similar to a Scrabble game as shown in the figure below.

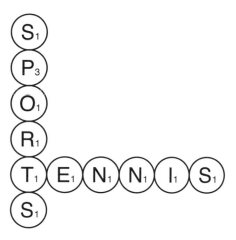

Adapted, by permission from CIRA, *50 games with 50 tennis balls.* ©2003 CIRA Ontario.

To letter the balls, select the number of balls you have from the following table and letter them as indicated. For example, if you have 75 tennis balls, letter seven balls with an A, two balls with a B, and so on.

	Number of balls		
	50	**75**	**100**
A	5	7	9
B	2	2	2
C	1	2	3
D	2	3	4
E	6	9	12
F	1	1	2
G	2	2	3
H	1	2	2
I	5	7	9
J	0	0	1
K	1	1	1
L	2	3	4
M	1	2	2
N	3	4	6
O	4	6	9
P	1	2	2
Q	0	0	1
R	3	5	6
S	2	3	4
T	3	5	6
U	2	3	4
V	1	1	2
W	1	2	2
X	0	1	1
Y	1	2	2
Z	0	0	1

Group Juggling

Objectives

- To remember partners and prevent balls from hitting the ground
- To build teamwork

Players

Teams of three to seven players

Equipment

One ball per player

Setup

Each team stands in a circle and begins with one ball per circle.

Instructions

1. All players begin with their arms raised.
2. The person with the ball throws it across the circle to someone, keeping his arms raised.
3. That player catches the ball, then throws it to another person who has her arms raised. After catching and throwing the ball, each player then lowers his arms. This way the group knows who still needs to receive the ball.
4. All players must remember the player to whom they threw the ball.
5. The last person with arms raised passes the ball back to the first thrower, who still has his arms raised.
6. Continue passing the ball in the same order.
7. The game ends when someone drops a ball.
8. See how many times the group can successfully pass the ball to the whole group.

Tips and Variations

- Add another ball each time the ball successfully goes around the circle, until each player has a ball. Then see how many times the team can pass all of the balls without dropping any.
- Also increase the distance between players or specify specific passes or ways to catch the ball that make the game more difficult.

Catch 'Em All

Objective

To work together to catch as many balls as possible

Players

Teams of two to eight players

Equipment

- Fifty tennis balls
- One towel, blanket, or tarp per group

Setup

- Teams distribute themselves around their towel or blanket and raise it to about waist height.
- The leader places 10 to 15 balls on each towel or blanket.

Instructions

1. Players toss the balls at least six feet (2 m) into the air and then try to catch as many balls as possible.
2. See which group can catch the most balls.
3. Each group retrieves their balls and tries to beat their highest score.

Tips and Variations

- Start with one ball and build to as many balls as possible.
- Use a tarp or parachute and work together as a large group to try to toss and catch all 50 balls.
- Two small groups pass the balls to each other.

Dunk It

Objectives

- To dunk as many balls as possible within a time limit
- To learn to make accurate bounce passes

Players

Teams of three to five players

Equipment

- Two containers
- Fifty numbered balls
- Two pylons

Setup

- Put one container at each end of the playing area. Designate one container as even and the other as odd.
- Place a pylon approximately five paces in front of each container.
- Put the balls between the two pylons.
- Designate a starting line 10 paces from the pylon.

Instructions

1. Each team lines up behind the starting line. On the *go* signal, the first player from each team runs to retrieve any ball. If the number on the ball is even, the player runs toward the even container and, from the pylon, tries to bounce the ball into the container. If successful, he scores a point. If unsuccessful, he returns the ball to the playing area for someone else to retrieve and goes to the back of his line. The next person in line goes to find a ball and tries to dunk it (bounce it into the container).
2. Players continue to try to score as many points as they can within a certain amount of time set by the leader.

Tips and Variations

- All players go at the same time.
- Vary the distance and type of throw.
- Try it as a three-legged exercise with partners.

Ambulance Relay

Objectives

- To carry as many balls on top of a gym mat across the playing area as possible
- To build teamwork skills

Players

Teams of two to four players

Equipment

- Ten to thirty balls per team
- One gym mat per team

Setup

- Establish a starting line and place each team's gymnastics mat and tennis balls at the line.
- Establish a turning line from which the group returns to the starting line.
- Line up the teams near their mat and tennis balls.

Instructions

1. Players hold onto the sides of the mat and try to carry a tennis ball on top of the mat to the other end of the gym and back.
2. If a ball falls off, the group tries again from the starting line.
3. If the group successfully carries one tennis ball, they try two, then three, and so on.
4. After the specified playing time elapses, the leader gives the signal to stop. The team carrying the most tennis balls is the winner.

Tips and Variations

50 Tennis Ball Race: Start with 50 balls on the mat. Time how long it takes the team to cross the gym. Add one second to the team's time for every dropped ball.

Load 'Em Up

Objective

To have fun loading up a teammate with as many balls as possible

Players

Teams of four to six players

Equipment

- Fifteen to twenty tennis balls per team
- One bucket per team

Setup

- Each team designates a holder.
- Designate a starting line, and a place for the holders approximately 10 paces away from the starting line.
- Teams line up behind the starting line, and the holders stand in their place in front of their team.

X4 X3 X2 X1 | Y

Instructions

1. Give each team a bucket containing 15 to 20 tennis balls. On the go signal, the first player on the team (X1) takes the ball to the holder (Y) and returns to the end of the line.
2. The second player (X2) on the team takes a ball to the holder and returns to the end of the line. The process continues until the holder is holding all the balls or until she drops one.
3. The team with the holder who can support the most balls is the winner. The holder cannot use her pockets or create pockets in her clothing to hold the tennis balls.

Tips and Variations

Once the holder has all the balls, she must make her way back to her team without dropping them.

Sitting Duck

Objective

To score points for your team and avoid being a sitting duck

Players

Any number of players, divided into two to four teams.

Equipment

- Pinnies to designate teams
- One numbered ball per player

Setup

Each player has a numbered tennis ball and stands randomly in the playing area.

Instructions

1. On the leader's command, players throw their ball into the air at least nine feet (3 m).
2. Players try to catch someone else's ball before it hits the ground.
3. If they catch the ball in flight, they remain standing. If they catch it off a bounce, they sit down.
4. The instructor calls out a number.
5. The person with that number, if standing, must keep his feet where they are and try to hit a sitting duck from the other team (who must remain stationary) by rolling a ball at her. If he hits an opponent's sitting duck, he scores a point for his team.
6. A new round begins. If the leader calls a person's number who is a sitting duck, then a new round begins.

Tips and Variations

The more teams there are, the easier it is to find a target to hit.

Tennis Ball Relay

Objective

To collect as many tennis balls as possible for your team

Players

Teams of three to five players

Equipment

Fifty to one hundred numbered tennis balls

Setup

- Place the teams at one end of the field or gym.
- Distribute the balls throughout the playing area.

Instructions

1. On the go signal, the first player from each team rushes to get a ball and returns to tag the second player, who rushes to get another ball. The pattern continues until all the balls are gone.
2. When all the balls have been retrieved, the team that has collected the most balls wins.

Tips and Variations

Number the teams. Players are allowed to pick up only balls that end with their number. For example, team three can only pick up balls numbered 3, 13, 23, 33, 43, and so on.

Shuttle Run

Objective

To run with a ball through the course

Players

Teams of three or four players

Equipment

- Three tennis balls per team
- Three hula hoops per team

Setup

- Designate a baseline.
- For each team, set up three hoops in a line, with each hoop progressively farther from the baseline (about two to three paces apart). Place one tennis ball in each hoop.
- Each team lines up at the baseline.

Instructions

1. On the *go* signal, the first person on each team runs to the first hoop, grabs a tennis ball, runs back to the baseline, and places the ball on the line. The player then runs to the second hoop and returns to the baseline with the ball, then runs to the third hoop and returns to the baseline with the ball.
2. When the first player has retrieved all three balls, she returns them one at a time in the reverse order: returning the farthest ball first.
3. When the first player has replaced the balls, she sits down, and the second player starts. Continue this pattern with each player.
4. The first team to finish, with all players seated, wins.

Tips and Variations

- Place four balls in each hoop. Run this game as a relay, with each player getting one ball at a time. Teams should strategize so that their fastest runner picks up the balls from the farthest hoops.
- This is a fun way to do basketball "suicide" runs.

Clean Your Room

Objective

To quickly throw balls out of your area into the opponent's area

Players

Two teams of any number of players

Equipment

- At least 50 numbered tennis balls
- A wall

Setup

Separate the playing area into two halves with a dividing wall or curtain that can be opened a couple yards at one end. Assign each team to half the playing area and give the teams an equal number of balls.

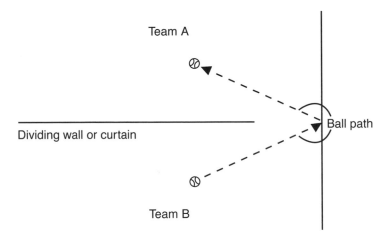

Team A

Dividing wall or curtain

Ball path

Team B

Adapted, by permission from CIRA, *50 games with 50 tennis balls.* ©2003 CIRA Ontario.

Instructions

1. On the leader's command, players rid their area of balls by throwing them over the dividing wall or curtain and off the far wall so that they bounce safely into the opponent's area.

2. When the designated time has elapsed, the leader signals, the players stop, and the balls are counted. The team with the fewest balls in their area is the winner.

Tips and Variations

- Safety tip: The balls must be bounced off a wall to avoid hitting people.
- Total the number of points written on the balls.

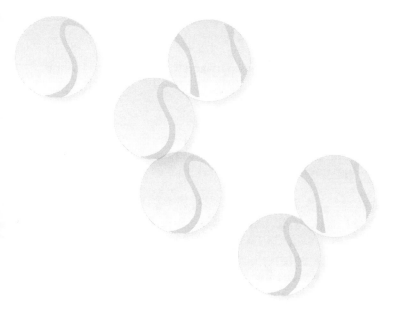

Toss-and-Run Tag

Objectives

- To mix up balls so that being called It is a surprise
- To practice tossing and catching

Players

Any number of players

Equipment

- Fifty numbered tennis balls
- Music and music player

Setup

Players scatter throughout the playing area, each with a numbered tennis ball in her hand.

Instructions

1. The leader starts the music to start the game. Players make eye contact with someone and toss the ball to that person to switch balls. Switching continues with other players until the music stops.
2. When the music stops, the leader calls out a number (or a few numbers). The player with that number is It. The new It shouts, "I'm It! I'm It!" and tries to tag as many people as possible.
3. Tagged players jog around the outside of the playing area until the game is restarted. Restart the game frequently to identify a new It.

Tips and Variations

- Predetermine a task instead of jogging for players to do when tagged.
- When you call out a number to be It, also state the corresponding activity from the following list. The tagged players must do 10 reps of the fitness task assigned to that number before rejoining the game. (See the following Fifty Fitness Activities; 1-26 are lettered for use in alphabet games.)

Fifty Fitness Activities

1A. Jumping jacks: Hands down, feet together, then jump with hands up and feet apart, then jump back to the starting position.

2B. Tuck jumps: Jump and bring the knees to the chest while jumping.

3C. Stride jumps: One foot goes forward and the other back, jump, and reverse feet.

4D. Push-ups: Flat on the floor, facedown, push body up with arms.

5E. Sit-ups: Lie on back, knees bent, slide hands to knees.

6F. Wall sits: Sit against a wall as if sitting on a chair.

7G. Arm punches: Alternate punches with both hands.

8H. Leg kicks: Kick as if kicking a football.

9I. Speed run on the spot: Run fast in place.

10J. Gluteal kicks: Run in place with heels contacting your butt.

11K. Log rolls: Lie flat on the ground and roll over.

12L. Front rolls: Somersault forward on the ground.

13M. Back rolls: Somersault backward on the ground.

14N. Arm curls: Hands down and pull up to shoulder by bending at the elbow.

15O. Arm-press isometrics: Push hands together and hold for 10 seconds.

16P. Arm-pull isometrics: Pull hands apart and hold for 10 seconds.

17Q. Right-foot hops: Hop on right foot.

18R. Left-foot hops: Hop on left foot.

19S. Stork balances: Stand stationary on one foot.

20T. Two-foot hops: Hop on both feet for 10 seconds.

21U. Leap frogs: Hands on the ground in crouch position, hop forward and land on feet and hands.

22V. Lunge jumps: One foot forward and the other back, front knee bent about 90 degrees, jump and switch legs.

23W. Lunge walk: One foot forward and the other back, front knee bent about 90 degrees, take step moving the back foot forward and bend the knee to about 90 degrees.

24X. Shoulder rolls: Roll shoulders forward five times, backward five times.

25Y. Skip on the spot: Ten skips with a rope or imaginary rope.

26Z. Ski jump: Hop side to side.

27. Crunches: Lie on back and bring knees to elbows.

28. Forearm push-ups: With forearms on the ground, do a push-up.

29. V-sits: Sit on the ground, lift both legs and bring chest to legs.

30. Hand-clap push-ups: Do a push-up and clap hands before catching yourself again with your hands.

31. March steps: March in place.

32. Mountain climbers: Reach up with alternating hands and feet.

33. Squats: Squat down, touch the ground, stand back up.

34. Trunk twists: Stand and twist upper body to both sides.

35. Toe touches: Stand and then bend down to touch toes.

36. Crab walk: With back to ground, walk on feet and hands.

37. Neck-lateral-flexion stretch: Stretch neck to the side.

38. Shoulder-abduction stretch: Stretch arms behind back.

39. Shoulder-rotation stretch: Grasp towel behind back.

40. Shoulder-flexion stretch: Place arms over head against wall.

41. Back-rotation stretch: Lie on floor, cross right leg over left, then switch leg positions.

42. Back-lateral-flexion stretch: Stand and slide right arm down toward right knee, then left arm toward left knee.

43. Back-flexion stretch: Lie on back, use hands to bring both knees to chest.

44. Gastrocnemius stretch: Lean toward wall, keeping back leg straight and allowing front knee to bend.

45. Soleus stretch: Lean toward wall, keeping back leg slightly bent and allowing front knee to bend.

46. Quadriceps stretch: Pull ankle gently toward your butt.

47. Hamstring stretch: Lie on floor, pull one knee toward chest, then switch and pull other knee toward chest.

48. Hip-abduction: Kneel on floor, pull right leg up and out away from the body, then switch legs.

49. Hip-adduction: Kneel on the floor, pull right knee toward left side of chest, then switch sides.

50. Back-cat stretch: Kneel on floor, drop head and raise back.

Sockey

Objective

To score on hockey nets with a tennis ball in a combination of floor hockey and soccer

Players

Two teams of four to seven players

Equipment

- Two hockey nets (or four pylons)
- One tennis ball

Setup

- Place two floor hockey nets (or two pylons, two paces apart) at opposite ends of a gym or outdoor playing area.
- Both teams start on their half of the playing area, and one of the goalies is given the ball to start the game (play rock, paper, scissors to determine who starts with the ball; see chapter 7 for instructions on how to play rock, paper, scissors).

Instructions

1. Play floor hockey with a tennis ball, but advance play by kicking the ball.
2. Hands can be used to put the ball down but not to advance the ball forward (except by the goalie). If the ball is advanced after it touches a player's hands, the other team gets the ball.
3. Play for a specified time; the team that scores the most goals is the winner.

Tips and Variations

This is a great and easy pickup game for recess or other breaks.

Chapter 4

© John Byl

Dollar Store Games

For most teachers and recreation leaders, dollar stores are probably one of the "professional" stores they visit most often. These stores offer many neat things for a small amount of money. These stores are a great resource for equipment for enjoyable physical activities, and several of the games involving such equipment also work with letters and literacy. We have had fun recording these games and inventing a few others. We know you will have even more fun playing these games, developing variations, and creating totally new games with materials from the shelves of the dollar store.

The games and illustrations in this chapter are adapted, by permission, from CIRA, *Bang for your buck.* ©2004 CIRA Ontario. Unless otherwise noted, the photos in this chapter are reprinted, by permission, from CIRA, *Bang for your buck.* ©2004 CIRA Ontario.

INTERLOCKING FOAM SQUARES

These inexpensive squares provide lots of opportunities. To get started, they provide a pathway for students to walk on and discover ways of moving. They can be assembled into cubes with numbers or activities written on each face to direct the next exercise, or the cubes can provide a safety spot in a game of tag.

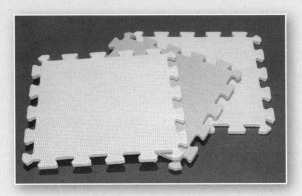

Bog Walk

Objective

To work as a group to discover the secret path required to move across the squares

Players

Groups of 8 to 12 players

Equipment

- Approximately 36 interlocking foam squares
- One piece of paper and one pencil per group

Setup

- The leader creates a square pattern using the interlocking squares.
- Determine a secret path across the squares. Write it down but do not show the players.

Instructions

1. Players line up and take turns trying to identify the path through trial and error, with one player on the grid at a time. The players begin at one edge of the grid.

2. If a player steps onto a square that is a part of the path, the leader calls out "squish." This means that the player is safe and can take another step, moving forward, to the side, backward, or diagonally.

3. If the player steps onto a square that is not a part of the path, the leader calls out "EEEEEEEH," or imitates a buzzer sound. The player moves to the back of the line and the next player tries.

4. Team members who are watching can assist the player on the grid with verbal suggestions, helping him find the correct path.

5. The game is over when every player has made it through the grid as quickly as possible.

6. Give players time to discuss and plan between turns or before they begin another game with a new sheet with a new secret path.

Tips and Variations

Silent Breadcrumbs: Play the same way, but players cannot talk to each other.

Sample secret pathway across the grid

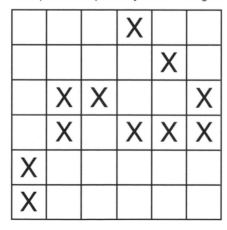

Fitness Frolics

Objective

To complete different fitness activities

Players

Teams of four to six players

Equipment

- Twelve interlocking foam squares assembled to form two dice
- One marker to write on foam squares

Setup

- On the interlocking foam squares that form the first die, write out a variety of fitness challenges. For example, sit-ups × 2, stride jumps × 2, push-ups × 2, balance × 5 seconds, jumping jacks × 3, running on the spot × 5 seconds. On the other die, write the numerals 1 through 6, just like on a normal die.
- Place the dice in the center of the playing area.

Instructions

1. The first player on each team runs to the center of the playing area and rolls the dice. Her team must then complete the activity. For example, if stride jumps × 2 is rolled on the one die, and a 4 is rolled on the other die, multiply 4 times 2 to determine the number of times an activity is done. In this case, each member of the team must complete eight stride jumps.

2. The activity ends when everyone from each team has had a chance to roll the dice.

Tips and Variations

• Class Dice Challenge: The leader rolls the dice and the entire class does the challenge.

• Opposition: Players roll activities for a different team.

• Race Time: The first team to complete all six challenges on the dice wins. Team members must complete every challenge, and if they roll the same activity twice, they must do it twice before rolling again.

• Assign letters for activities. On the activity die, replace the activities with the letters A through F, and make a corresponding chart listing activities. This allows you to change the activities periodically according to a sport of focus or skill level.

Stepping-Stones

Objectives

- To be the first team to safely cross the playing area
- To develop problem-solving and teamwork skills

Players

Teams of four to six players

Equipment

One interlocking foam square per player

Setup

- Divide the group into teams, and give one foam square to each player.
- Define a shoreline (starting line) and line up the teams behind it.
- Designate an end line that they need to reach.

Instructions

1. On the *go* signal, each team must travel across the playing area by using the foam squares as stepping-stones. The players may stand only on shore or on the stepping-stones. The players do not need to interlock the stepping-stones and can pick them up and move them when necessary.
2. Players are not allowed to touch the floor. If a player touches the ground, her whole team must go back to the starting line or perform a specified activity before they may continue.
3. The first team to reach the other side is the winner.

Tips and Variations

Expert Version: Reduce the number of foam squares. The fewer foam squares needed, the more successful the group.

Square Tag

Objective

To avoid being tagged by briefly standing on a foam-square safe haven

Players

Five to fifty-five players

Equipment

One foam square per five players

Setup

- Toss the foam squares throughout the playing area.
- Designate one to four players as It.

Instructions

1. On the *go* signal, the group starts playing tag. Players are safe when touching a foam square and can remain on a square for five seconds (counting *1 steamboat, 2 steamboat* or counting *1 one thousand, 2 one thousand*). After five seconds, players must leave the foam square and cannot return to the same safe haven without going to another one first.
2. If a player is tagged, he becomes It.

Tips and Variations

- Activity Tag: When a player is tagged, she does not become It. Instead, she goes to the side of the gym and performs a specified exercise, such as running a lap around the gym, push-ups, or sit-ups. The leader changes Its frequently.
- Stay Tag: Divide the players into two groups, and play two separate games. When a player is tagged he joins the other game. The objective of the game is to remain in the same game as long as possible.

PLAYING CARDS

If you live near a casino, ask about getting used decks of cards for free. At dollar stores you can often buy extra-large decks, which are fun for playing group games. Don't forget that you can also make a deck of large cards using bristol board or poster board and colored markers.

© Human Kinetics

Moving Seats

Objectives

- To move the most number of times during the game
- To become comfortable with other players

Players

At least 10 players

Equipment

- One chair per player
- One or two decks of playing cards

Setup

- Place the chairs in a tight circle with very little space between them.
- Give each player a card and ask players to remember the suit.
- Cards are returned to the leader.

Instructions

1. The leader turns over cards from the deck one at a time and shows them to the group. If a player's card is the same suit as the card that is showing, she may move one chair to the right. If that chair is occupied, she must sit on the lap of the player on it. Players may only move if no one is sitting on their lap. Players must keep track of how many times they move during the game.

2. After the leader shows a predetermined number of cards, the person who moved the most times is the winner.

Tips and Variations

- Safety tip: Be sure the chairs are sturdy.
- Pileup Moving Seats: Players may move even if someone is on their lap. If a player is at the bottom of a pile, he takes his stack of people with him and moves to the top of the pile. If he's in the middle, he takes everyone above him.

BRACELETS

The games in this section use bracelets. Bracelets or sweatbands are great for identifying teams, especially in sports like basketball and European handball where players often have their arms up. You can also use hair elastics instead of bracelets, especially for younger players with smaller wrists.

© Human Kinetics

Bracelet Ball

Objective

To encourage team play in a regular sport or game. Many leaders and instructors experience the frustration of seeing a small number of players dominate a game, whether it is floor hockey, soccer, basketball, or any other team sport. By using bracelets, you can encourage more passing and teamwork.

Players

The number of players appropriate for the sport

Equipment

- Two or three bracelets per player
- Sport-specific equipment

Setup

- Designate teams as appropriate for the game being played, e.g., basketball, floor hockey, soccer.
- Give each player two or three bracelets at the beginning of the game.

Instructions

1. Each time a player scores, she must remove a bracelet. If she has no more bracelets, she is no longer allowed to score. Instead, she passes to help her teammates score.
2. Keep track of the score by counting the bracelets that have been removed.

Tips and Variations

Hand out more bracelets to reward great passing or team play so that active players do not get frustrated.

Bracelet Tag

Objective

To collect as many bracelets as possible

Players

Any number of players

Equipment

Three bracelets per player

Setup

All players start with three bracelets on their arms and scatter themselves throughout the playing area.

Instructions

1. Everybody is It, and they all try to tag each other.
2. If a player is tagged, both players kneel on the ground and the one who was tagged gives a bracelet to the player who tagged him. When players are kneeling to exchange bracelets, they cannot be tagged.
3. If two players tag each other at the same time, they play a game of rock, paper, scissors to determine who gets the bracelet (see chapter 7 for instructions on how to play rock, paper, scissors).
4. A player may continue playing even after running out of bracelets.

Tips and Variations

- Second-Chance Tag: The players can play any tag game. Give each player two bracelets and designate an It. When a player is tagged, he gives the player who is It a bracelet and is free again. When a player without a bracelet is tagged, she becomes the new It.

- Movement Tag: Have students move in different locomotor patterns; e.g., hop, skip, gallop, or march; while playing Bracelet Tag.

- Rock, Paper, Scissors Tag: When a player tags someone, they play rock, paper, scissors for the bracelet. This alleviates some of the competitiveness of the game.

- Color Tag: Give each player one bracelet. Players can only tag players with a bracelet of the same color. If a player has no bracelet, she can tag any player with a bracelet.

- Ultimate Tag: When a player tags someone, he gets all of that person's bracelets. The player who was tagged goes to the side of the playing area and runs on the spot until the game is over. Whoever has all the bracelets at the end wins.

STUFFED ANIMALS

Because homes with children generally have a plentiful supply of stuffed animals, you may not have to go to the dollar store for the equipment in these games. Simply borrow the stuffed animals from friends or ask the players to bring them from home.

Animal Keeper

Objective

To pass an animal 15 consecutive times as a team

Players

Teams of three to six players

Equipment

One stuffed animal per two teams

Setup

- Divide the playing area into two-pasture (two adjacent squares) blocks. (A badminton court is a good size for teams of three players, while a volleyball court works well for teams of six players.)
- Divide the group into teams and assign two teams to each two-pasture block, one team per pasture.
- Give these two teams one stuffed animal.

- All the members of one team stand in a scattered formation in their pasture with the animal.
- Two players from the other team stand in their own pasture. The other members are hunters and stand in the first team's pasture.

Instructions

1. On the go signal, the team with the stuffed animal attempts to pass it from player to player, making 15 consecutive passes.
2. The player holding the animal cannot move, but can pivot on one foot.
3. If a player drops the animal or if the player holding the animal takes a step, she gives the animal to the other team in their pasture.
4. If a team is successful, its members can see how many times they can complete 15 consecutive passes.
5. The other team's hunters try to intercept a pass without touching the opposing players.
6. When a hunter intercepts a pass, she passes it to her teammate in her own team's pasture, and then all the hunters join their team and try to throw 15 consecutive passes.
7. The other team then sends their hunters to try to intercept a pass (all their players except the two who stay behind).

Tips and Variations

Animal Roundup: Four teams play in the same area and each team has a stuffed animal. Each player with an animal has five seconds to pass the animal to a teammate. At the same time, players also try to intercept passes from other teams. Once a team has control of three stuffed animals, they win.

HOOPS

When most kids encounter a hula hoop they will try to see how long they can swing it around their hips (the world record is just less than 100 hours). However, hoops also provide great snake pits and dog pounds. When players try to quickly move into a hoop, make sure they are careful not to step on the hoop, which can cause them to slide and fall.

Snake Pit

Objective

To get back to the nest before being caught by the snake

Players

Ten to thirty players

Equipment

- Five hoops
- Upbeat music
- Music player

Setup

- Select a player to be the snake. The rest of the players are rats.
- Place one hoop in the middle of the playing area to serve as the snake hole. Spread the rest of the hoops throughout the playing area to serve as rat nests.
- Assign each rat a home in one of the rat nests. Assign a roughly equal number of players to each hoop.

Instructions

1. The snake sits in her hole and closes her eyes.
2. When the music plays, the rats leave their nests and dance around the snake hole.
3. When the music stops, the snake chases the rats, attempting to tag them before they reach their specific nests.
4. If tagged, the rat joins the snake; now there are two snakes.
5. With all the rats in their hoops, the snakes go back to their pit, the music begins, and the game continues until all the rats are caught.

Tips and Variations

- Safety tip: Place the hoops away from the walls.
- Locomotion Snake Pit: Change the mode of movement, e.g., snakes have to slide on their feet, rats have to walk on all fours, and so on.

Dogcatcher

Objective

To avoid being tagged and put in the dog pound

Players

Ten to thirty players

Equipment

- A recording of the song "Who Let the Dogs Out?" (originally sung by Baha Men)
- Music player
- Six to eight hoops
- Two to four pool noodles to use as tagging sticks

Setup

- Scatter the hoops throughout the playing area. Each hoop is a dog pound.
- Designate two to four players to be dogcatchers. The rest of the players are dogs.

Instructions

1. When the music starts, the dogcatchers try to tag the dogs with the tagging sticks.
2. If tagged, the player must stand in the dog pound. The player must stay in the dog pound until another player frees him. Players free a tagged player by raising the hoop over the tagged player's head without getting tagged themselves.
3. There can be a maximum of three players in each dog pound at a time. When the fourth dog arrives, whoever was in the dog pound first gets to leave. Players leave in the order they arrived.
4. Stop the music frequently to change dogcatchers.

Tips and Variations

Safety tip: Dogcatchers may tag dogs from the shoulders down only.

SPONGES

Sponges can be used in a variety of games. They are great objects to throw and catch because they are soft and can be used instead of beanbags. Players can also balance them on their head.

Asteroids

Objectives

To avoid being tagged and to help others get back into the game

Players

Any number of players

Equipment

Two sponge pieces per player

Setup

- Designate one to three players to be It.
- Give the rest of the players two asteroids (sponge pieces) each. Players may never have more than two asteroids during the game.
- Players scatter themselves throughout the playing area.

Instructions

1. Players place the two sponges on their head. At the go signal, they move around to avoid being tagged.

2. The first time a player is tagged, he must drop one of his asteroids. If he is tagged again, he must drop his other asteroid and then explode (jump up, then land and remain in a squatting position) until another player tosses him an asteroid and he places it on his head. He can then rejoin the game.

3. If players drop an asteroid as they walk, they cannot pick it up. If they drop both, they must explode.

4. Players can pick up another player's asteroid from the floor and throw it to someone in the squatting position. They can only toss to a squatted player.

5. This game is great for building social skills and team play. Encourage players to work together to ensure that no one remains in the exploded position for more than 20 seconds.

Tips and Variations

- Safety tip: If playing in a limited space, require players to speed-walk instead of run.

- Exercise Asteroids: If a player loses both her asteroids, she can go to a designated area and perform a fitness exercise to collect two more pieces.

Sponge Ball

Objectives

To hit other players with sponges and to avoid getting hit

Players

Any number of players

Equipment

One sponge per player

Setup

Players stand in a scattered formation throughout the playing area, each holding a sponge (or scatter the sponges randomly around the playing area).

Instructions

1. On the go signal, the sponge-ball fight begins.
2. Players throw sponges at other players, trying to hit them below the waist. Players run around the playing area and pick up sponges from the floor and continue throwing.
3. When hit, players do 10 jumping jacks (or another exercise) before returning to the pandemonium.

Tips and Variations

None

ALPHABET FOAM PUZZLES

These little foam letters provide great incentive for reaching goals in a game. And they help reinforce literacy while playing games.

Letter Tag

Objectives

To avoid being tagged and to perform an exercise to resume the game after being tagged

Players

Any number of players

Equipment

- One alphabet foam puzzle
- One activity chart (made by the leader)

Setup

- Before the game begins, make a chart that lists an activity for each letter of the alphabet and tape it to the wall. Refer to the first 26 activities in "Fifty Fitness Activities" on pages 105-106.

- Put all the letters from the alphabet puzzle into a bucket or bag near the wall chart
- Designate two players as It.
- All other players are in a scattered formation inside the playing area.

Instructions

1. Play a game of tag.
2. When a player is tagged, he goes to the bucket or bag, picks a letter, looks at it, returns it to the bucket or bag, then goes to a chart on the wall and performs the activity that corresponds with the letter he selected. The player then returns to the game.
3. Change Its often.

Tips or Variations

None

Alphabet Backboard Ball

Objective

To be the first team to complete the puzzle

Players

Two teams of four to eight players

Equipment

- Six to eight Gator balls
- Two alphabet puzzles

Setup

- Divide the players into two teams.
- Assign each team to one half of a basketball court.
- Place a blank puzzle on the sideline for each team.
- Place all the letters in a pile at the center line.
- Players start on their court and a leader tosses each team three or four Gator balls.

Instructions

1. On the *go* signal, players try to hit the other team's backboard with the Gator ball.
2. Players can take only three steps or hold the ball for five seconds before passing or shooting it.
3. If a player hits the backboard, she gets to pick a letter from the pile of letters on the side, and place it in the puzzle for her team. Players can take only one letter at a time.
4. If the player takes a letter that the team already has, he has to put it back but does not get to take another letter.
5. The first team to complete its puzzle wins.

Tips and Variations

- Individual Alphabet Backboard Ball: Play with two teams, but each player works independently to spell his or her name the fastest.
- Word Scramble Backboard Ball: After playing and collecting letters for a certain number of minutes, teams must make as many words as possible with the letters they have collected. Each team can select two free "bonus letters" to help them make additional words.

Rock, Paper, Scissors
Mad Scramble

Objective

To collect the first three letters of your first name and first three letters of your last name as quickly as possible

Players

Any number of players

Equipment

Five to ten foam alphabet puzzles

Setup

- Place all the letters from the alphabet puzzles in a pile at one end of the playing area.
- Players scatter themselves around the pile of letters.

Instructions

1. Players move around the gym playing rock, paper, scissors (see chapter 7 for details) with each other. Paper covers rock, rock smashes scissors, and scissors cuts paper. When a player wins a game, he goes to the pile of letters and finds a letter in his name.
2. Players continue to play rock, paper, scissors, picking up a letter with every win.
3. The first player to pick up the first three letters of her first name and first three letters of her last name is the winner.

Tips and Variations

Team Scramble: Divide the group into teams and have players challenge someone from the other team. Players select any letter they want when they win at rock, paper, scissors. When a signal is given, team members combine their letters to form as many words as they can.

BALLS

The wacky balls referred to in this section are balls that are not perfectly round, but have bumps and edges. These balls act as equalizers, because a player who is skilled in a traditional sport has no more experience with wacky balls than someone with no athletic experience. Beach balls are also effective for changing familiar games or creating new ones. Another great ball that is totally safe, totally unpredictable, and totally fun is the bladder of an old soccer ball, basketball, or volleyball. Feel free to substitute a beach ball for any of the wacky ball games.

© Human Kinetics

Wacky Ball

Objective

To score as many baskets as possible

Players

Two, four, or six teams of four to eight players each

Equipment

- Colored pinnies to distinguish the teams, one per player
- At least 10 rubber wacky balls
- Four to six basketball hoops

Setup

- Divide players into two, four, or six teams and assign each a basket to defend. Teams stand near their basket while waiting to start the game.
- Place a container of wacky balls in the center of the gym or randomly scatter the balls around the playing area.
- You can use pails or garbage cans instead of basketball hoops.

Instructions

1. This is a fun, fast-paced basketball variation that encourages passing. Small wacky balls are perfect because the balls' bounce is unpredictable.
2. When the game begins, teams try to score on other baskets while trying to defend their own.
3. Players may run to get a ball, but once they have a ball, they must stand still. Balls can be moved only by bounce passing.
4. Shots may only be made by players standing in the basketball key or a designated scoring area.
5. After a designated time, the leader stops the game, and the team with the best score wins.

Tips and Variations

Plus–minus: Keep track of baskets a team makes and subtract the number of baskets made against them. The team with the best plus–minus score is the winner.

In and Out

Objective

To work cooperatively to try and get as many players as possible to move in and stand against a wall and then run back out without being hit by the ball

Players

Ten to twenty players

Equipment

- One leg of a pair of pantyhose
- One rubber ball

Setup

- Place the rubber ball in the nylon stocking.
- Designate a swinger, who has his back to the wall, holding the nylon. He swings it so that the ball alternates bouncing off the wall on his right side and then his left side, far away from him in a steady motion, about waist high. He continues regardless of what the other players are doing.
- In front of the swinger are two equal lines of players, standing near the swinger but far enough away that they do not get hit by the ball.

© John Byl

Instructions

1. One by one, when a player senses that there is an opening, she runs to stand next to the player at the wall, with the ball hitting the wall on the other side of her.

2. Players from each line run in one at a time and stand next to the player with the nylon and ball. Eventually, there will be a line of 5 to 10 players against the wall on each side.

3. Once everyone has gotten in without anyone being hit by the ball, the players must take turns running out again.

4. If a player is hit by the ball, he becomes the swinger.

5. The group tries to get as many players as they can against the wall.

Tips and Variations

When running toward the wall, players should be careful not to trip and fall into the wall.

Crazy Hot Potato

Objectives

To avoid being stuck with the "hot potato" and to do various silly activities

Players

Groups of about 10

Equipment

- One wacky ball for each group
- Fast-paced music
- Music player

Setup

- Players in each group sit in a circle.
- Give each group a hot potato (ball).

Instructions

1. When the music starts, the group passes the hot potato around the circle until the music stops. The player holding the ball when the music stops must stand up and do a short activity, such as two jumping jacks, and then sit back down. Players can select an activity or you can refer them to a chart such as the one on pages 105-106.

2. The game continues, and every time that player touches the ball, she must stand up and do her activity.

3. The music stops again, and the player with the hot potato must choose another activity (e.g., a forward roll). Now two people are doing an activity every time they touch the ball.

4. Continue until everyone in the group has been stuck with the hot potato and everyone is doing a silly activity.

Tips and Variations

None

TOWELS AND SCARVES

Towels are soft and strong enough to catch and propel objects or even to replace a bat in baseball when a lighter ball is used. Scarves are small and light enough that they flow like a dragon's tail. They are also useful as flags for tag games or even sports like flag football. These pieces of equipment add delightful energy that encourages players to run.

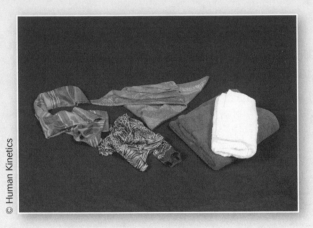

© Human Kinetics

Towel Baseball

Objective

To score as many runs as possible

Players

Two teams of 10 to 16 players

Equipment

- One towel for every two players
- One ball or stuffed animal
- Four bases for the ball diamond (folded towels work well)

Setup

- Divide the group into two teams.
- Set up a baseball diamond in the regular shape, but reduce the distance between bases by half.
- Instruct players that there is an invisible line running from first base to third base. If the ball does not cross this line, it is a foul ball.
- Send one team to the field, with pairs of players holding a towel between them to catch the ball or stuffed animal. The other team is behind home base waiting their turn to "bat."

Instructions

1. Two players go to home base at the same time. Each holds the end of the towel with a ball or stuffed animal on a towel. Together, they snap the towel to toss the ball into the playing field.
2. There are three ways to get out:
   a. If the ball is caught in the air, the batters are out. (Baseball rules apply for pop flies.)
   b. Runners who bat together must stay together at all times, with both holding their towel.
   c. If the runners are not touching their base when the batters have the ball, the runners are out.
3. There are no forced outs, and there can be numerous runners on any given base at any time. The inning is over when every pair has had a turn at bat.

Tips and Variations

Bat Towel: Play by regular baseball rules. Players use a Gator ball, and a towel with a knot tied at the end as a bat.

Dragon Tail

Objective

To steal other dragons' tails while keeping your own

Players

Four to six teams of any number of players

Equipment

One ribbon or scarf per team

Setup

- Divide the group into teams. Each team forms a dragon by putting their hands on the shoulders or waist of the player in front of them.
- The last player in line will tuck a ribbon or scarf into the back of his waistband.

Instructions

1. On the signal, the dragons try to steal the tails of other dragons while protecting their own tail.
2. If a dragon loses its tail or breaks apart, it is eliminated and goes to the sidelines to cheer on other dragons.
3. The objectives are to get the most tails and to be the last dragon alive.

Tips and Variations

- Dragon Exercises: The dragon stays in the game even if it loses its tail. When a team loses a tail, they go to the leader, who tells them what physical activity they must do to earn another tail, for example, run one lap of the playing area. Set a time limit, and the dragon with the most tails at the end of the game wins.
- Longest Dragon: When a dragon's tail is stolen, the front player leads his whole team to join the line of the dragon that tagged them. The player at the end is given the tail. The game ends when the entire group has formed one long dragon.

Scarf Tag

Objective

To take the "tails" off other players while keeping your own

Players

Any number of players

Equipment

One scarf per player

Setup

Give each player a scarf to tuck into the back of her waistband to form a tail. It can also be attached with a clothespin.

© Human Kinetics

Instructions

1. In this game of tag, everyone is It. Players try to steal each other's tails while keeping their own tail. When a player steals a tail, she tosses it to the tail-less player.

2. If a player's scarf is taken, he must take it to the leader. The player must then perform a designated activity, such as 20 jumping jacks or 10 sit-ups, before entering the game again. Change this activity often.

Tips and Variations

- Safety tip: Players should make sure their scarves are tucked in far enough that they don't pose a tripping hazard.

- Continuous Scarf Tag: When a player steals a scarf, she can kneel and tuck the second tail into her waistband next to the first one. A player who is kneeling cannot be tagged. See who can get the most tails by the end of the playing time.

POPSICLE STICKS

Popsicle sticks can be used in a variety of games in a variety of ways. Teams can use them to earn and tally points, which is a fun way to reinforce math skills. And in a game of tag, they become valuable, because when players are out of sticks, they're out of luck.

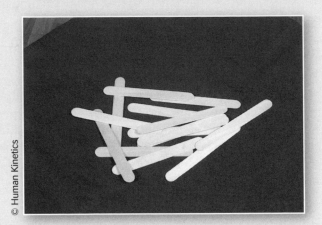

© Human Kinetics

Needle in the Haystack

Objective

To get as many points as possible for the team

Players

Teams of three players

Equipment

- Three numbered Popsicle sticks per player
- One container

Setup

- Collect all the sticks for the game and number them 1 through 10, repeating the sequence until all the sticks are numbered.
- Place the sticks in a container at one end of the playing area with the teams lined up at the other end.

Instructions

1. On the *go* signal, the first player from each team runs to the other end of the playing area, picks up one stick, and runs back.
2. The players continue picking up sticks either until a certain amount of time passes or all the sticks are gone.
3. The teams tally the points on their sticks, and the team with the most points wins.

Tips and Variations

For older players, write larger numbers that are more difficult to add. To make the mathematics more difficult, have players multiply the numbers on their sticks, but to keep this task reasonable, limit the number of sticks they pick up.

Three-Stick Tag

Objective

To keep as many sticks as possible

Players

Any number of players

Equipment

- Three Popsicle sticks per player
- Several containers to hold the sticks

Setup

- All players are It.
- Players scatter themselves throughout the playing area.
- Several containers are placed on various sides of the playing area.

Instructions

1. On the *go* signal, players start a game of tag.
2. If a player is tagged, he loses a stick by putting it in one of the containers or giving it to the leader.
3. If a player bumps into another player, both players lose a stick.
4. When a player loses all three sticks, he becomes a tree and must try to tag other players without moving his feet. If he is successful, the player he tagged must give him a stick, and then he can rejoin the game.

Tips and Variations

None

CONES AND PYLONS

Cones and pylons can be used to create light and quickly assembled goals, markers for relays, or boundary lines for games. The following games use them as a warm-up activity and as targets.

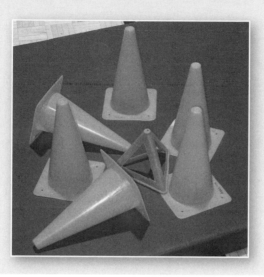

Up and Down

Objectives

Half of the players try to keep all the pylons upright, and the other half try to knock them over.

Players

Twenty to forty players

Equipment

Twenty to thirty minipylons

Setup

- Split the group into two teams.
- Randomly set half the pylons upright and half of them on their sides.

151

- Designate one team as the up team, and the other team as the down team.
- Players begin in a scattered position throughout the playing area.

Instructions

1. On the *go* signal, the up team runs to the pylons that are on their sides and puts them upright. The down team knocks over any pylons that are standing upright.

2. After a certain amount of time, stop the game and count how many pylons are up and how many are down. Declare a winner and then play another round, but switch roles.

Tips and Variations

Safety tips: Players can only use their hands to fix or knock down the pylons. They may not kick them. Players must be careful when bending down to touch a pylon so that they avoid hitting heads with another player.

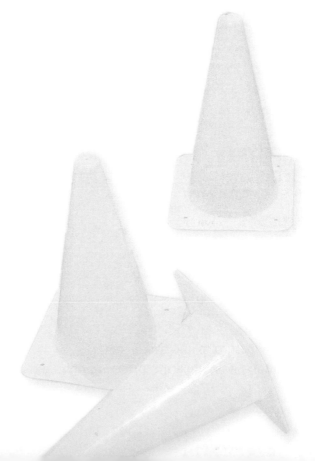

Ice Cream Topple

Objective

To knock a Wiffle ball off other players' pylons while protecting your own

Players

Twenty to forty players

Equipment

- Fifteen pylons
- Fifteen small Wiffle balls, beanbags, or tennis balls
- Fifteen Gator balls or other soft balls

Setup

- Scatter 15 ice cream cones (pylons) throughout the playing area, making sure they are not too close to one another.
- Assign each pylon to a player and have them place topping (a Wiffle ball) on each pylon.
- Players who do not have a pylon stand around the edge of the playing area.
- Balls are given to the players on the sidelines.

Instructions

1. Players stand by their pylons; they must stay within two steps of the pylon at all times, except as described in steps 7 and 8.
2. At the signal, players on the outside of the playing area roll the Gator balls and try to knock the Wiffle balls off the pylons. Players can use their hands, legs, and body to prevent balls from hitting their pylons.
3. If a player's Wiffle ball falls off, she picks it up and takes it to the player who rolled the ball. This player then takes her place on the playing area, putting the Wiffle ball back on top of the pylon.
4. Assign one or two players to roll the balls that are in the playing area back out.

5. As a leader, watch for players who are able to protect their pylons and keep the Wiffle ball from falling off for a long time. If you notice one, bring him to the attention of the other players so they can try extra hard to get his Wiffle ball. If he can still protect his pylon, you may want to encourage him to give his place to someone else.

6. A player cannot touch her Wiffle ball when protecting it. If she knocks it off herself, she must leave the playing area and give another player a turn.

7. A player guarding a pylon can roll a Gator ball to knock off another player's Wiffle ball. If this attempt is successful, the victim puts the Wiffle ball on the pylon, goes to the edge of the playing area, and leaves an unguarded pylon. This gives someone on the edge an easy target and a way to get into the playing area.

8. A player can leave her pylon to retrieve a ball, but must return to her pylon to roll it.

Tips and Variations

Safety tip: Encourage players to roll the ball underhand and to aim for the pylons and not other players.

Pylon Knock-Off

Objective

To knock opponents' pylons from their bench

Players

Two teams of 5 to 15 players

Equipment

- Two benches
- Twelve pylons
- Six or eight Gator balls

Setup

- Divide the playing area into two zones with a bench at the back of each zone (but not so far back that the weaker players have a difficult time throwing as far as the bench).
- Place six evenly spaced pylons on each bench. Mark off or establish a line around the bench that no defensive player may go into.
- Divide the players into two teams and give each team three or four balls.
- Players stand in a scattered formation in their zone.

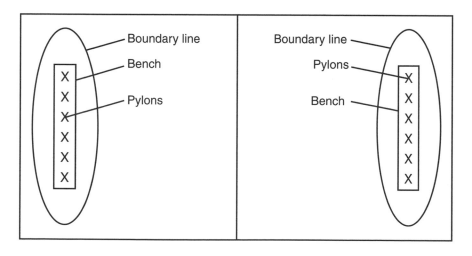

Instructions

1. At the signal, players throw the balls into the other team's zone, aiming to knock the pylons off the bench.

2. Players must stay in their half of the playing area, and defensive players must stay out of the marked area around their own bench.

3. The first team to knock half of the other team's pylons off the bench wins.

4. If the ball rebounds off a player who is trying to defend the pylons (players cannot throw the ball at players), that player must go to the side and do 25 jumping jacks before returning to the game. If the ball is caught by a player trying to defend the pylons, the thrower must go to the sidelines and do 25 jumping jacks before returning to the game.

Tips and Variations

None

BALLOONS

Balloons are a fun and inexpensive addition to your dollar store equipment. Balloons are lightweight and remind us of parties. They are a pure delight. Be sure to ask the group if anyone has a latex allergy, and avoid using latex balloons if anyone does.

Balloon Keep-Ups

Objective

To keep the balloon in the air using different body parts

Players

Groups of four to six players

Equipment

One inflated balloon for each group

Setup

Each group forms a circle and holds hands (except for one player at the beginning, who initiates the challenge by tossing the balloon into the air).

Instructions

1. Players are not allowed to let go of hands.
2. The leader calls out a body part (e.g., foot, elbow, head), and players must keep the balloon in the air only using that body part.
3. No player may hit the balloon two times in a row.
4. Players count the number of contacts made with the balloon for each body part.

Tips and Variations

None

Body-Part Balloon Tag

Objectives

- For pairs who are It to tag as many pairs as possible while supporting a balloon between their bodies
- For pairs who are not It to avoid being tagged while supporting a balloon between their bodies

Players

Any number of pairs

Equipment

One inflated balloon per pair

Setup

- Give each pair a balloon.
- Pairs scatter themselves throughout the playing area.

Instructions

1. The leader designates a body part, and players in the pair must hold the balloon between them using only that body part (e.g., head, hips, back).
2. Players may not touch the balloon with their hands once it is in place.
3. Two pairs of students are assigned to be It. These pairs must also support a balloon between their bodies.
4. If a pair is tagged, they become It.
5. If a balloon falls to the ground, the pair must do a brief fitness activity before continuing in the game. If the pair is tagged while doing the fitness activity, they become It when their activity is done.

Tips and Variations

Hot Air Balloon Tag: Players play regular tag but must keep a balloon in the air while moving around. If a player's balloon falls to the ground, she becomes It. This game can be played in pairs or individually.

Balloon Fitness

Objectives

To keep the balloons in the air and to perform the fitness activities written on balloons

Players

Any number of players

Equipment

- One inflated labeled balloon per player (see details in Setup section)
- Upbeat music
- Music player

Setup

- Write a different fitness activity on each balloon.
- Give each student a balloon, and begin to play music.

Instructions

1. When the music starts, players toss their balloon into the air. They move around the playing area, hitting any balloon near them, trying to keep the balloons in the air.
2. When the music stops, players take the balloon they hit last and perform the fitness activity written on it.
3. The leader starts the music and the game continues.

Tips and Variations

None

Activity Balloon Smash

Objective

To try to step on other players' balloons without letting anyone step on yours

Players

Any number of players

Equipment

- One inflated balloon per player
- String

Setup

Each player ties an inflated balloon to one of his or her ankles.

Instructions

1. On the signal to begin, players move around trying to step on other players' balloons.
2. If players' balloons are broken, then they must perform a designated activity while the others continue playing.
3. The last player with an inflated balloon wins.

Tips and Variations

Balloon Smash Stay: Players can keep playing when their balloon is smashed, but they must use their nondominant foot to step on balloons, and they are not allowed to run.

Balloon Tennis

Objective

To keep the balloon from landing on your side of the court

Players

Groups of two or four players

Equipment

- One inflated balloon per group
- Two pylons per group
- String
- Tape

Setup

- Separate the group into pairs.
- Tape the string on top of the pylons.

Instructions

1. Players establish their own boundary lines, keeping in mind the number of other games being played.
2. Players play rock, paper, scissors (see chapter 7) to determine who serves first. Serve by hitting the balloon upward over the net.
3. Players hit the balloon back and forth with a fist or open hand, trying to keep the balloon from hitting ground on their side of the net.
4. Players can hit the balloon only once on their side. However, you can increase this number for younger or less-skilled players.
5. Players score a point if the balloon lands in bounds in the opponent's side of the court or if the opponent's balloon lands out of bounds
6. The first player to score 10 points is the winner.

Tips and Variations

- Doubles Balloon Tennis: Play the same game in pairs, allowing two hits per side.
- Balloon Volleyball: Using a badminton net and court, play volleyball. Use the short service line as the end of the court. Another option is to play on a volleyball court, using the attack line as the end of the court.

CLOTHESPINS

Clothespins are an inexpensive and versatile addition to many games and activities. Players can easily attach them to clothing and easily take them off. Once they are clipped on clothes, kids are tempted to snatch them off one another. Therefore, a couple of games in this section require players to protect their clothespins. They also serve as a delightful tool for building towers and learning about group dynamics.

Everyone It

Objective

To get the most clothespins

Players

Any number of players

Equipment

Two clothespins per player

Setup

- Each player clips two clothespins on the back of his or her shirt.
- Define the playing area boundaries.
- Players scatter themselves throughout the playing area.

Instructions

1. At the signal to begin, players try to grab the clothespins off the backs of other players while staying within a designated playing area.
2. If a player gets a clothespin, she can kneel down and clip it to the back of her shirt. While she is kneeling, no one can remove her other clothespins.
3. Play for a specific amount of time.
4. When time is up, the person with the most clothespins wins.

Tips and Variations

Everyone It—Team Version: Play this game the same way, but divide players into two or more teams. Players try to get the clothespins from the backs of the players on the other team. At the end of the game, count each team's clothespins. The team with the most is the winner.

Tower Building

Objectives

- To build the highest clothespin tower
- To develop group dynamics

Players

Teams of four to six players

Equipment

Fifty clothespins per team

Setup

- Divide the players into teams. Teams of four to six people allow everyone to participate.
- Give each team 50 clothespins.

Instructions

1. Instruct the players to build the tallest tower they can in a certain amount of time.
2. Players may use only the clothespins they have been given. And they may not take the clothespins apart.
3. The team that builds the tallest freestanding tower wins.

Tips and Variations

- Stacked Tower: Play this game the same way, but teams may only stack the pins. The challenge is to see how many pins a team can stack before their tower falls over.
- The group dynamics that develop during this game are interesting to watch.

Guard the Belly Button

Objectives

- To steal the clothespins from the player who is It
- For the player who is It to prevent the clothespins from being stolen

Players

Groups of four to seven; each group plays independently

Equipment

- Three clothespins per group
- One pool noodle per group
- One blindfold per group

Setup

- Choose one player to be It. This player pins the clothespins to the front of his shirt, near his belly button.
- Blindfold the player who is It, and give him one large pool noodle.

Instructions

1. When the game starts, the players run up to the player who is It and try to remove a clothespin without letting It touch or hit them with the noodle.
2. If It touches a player, the tagged player must back up before trying again. You might have tagged players perform an activity before reentering the game, such as 10 sit-ups or 20 jumping jacks.
3. Play for two to three minutes.
4. Whoever steals the most clothespins wins the game. The player who is It wins if no one steals all the pins in the allotted time.

Tips and Variations

None

FRISBEES

Frisbees can put your games unit into flight. High-quality Frisbees can be quite expensive, but you can purchase inexpensive versions at the dollar store, allowing you to provide lots of fun for lots of players.

Frisbee Golf

Objective

To hit the targets with a Frisbee in the fewest throws

Players

- Up to 72 players
- No more than 18 groups of two to four players

Equipment

- One Frisbee per player
- One piece of paper and one pencil per team
- One list of targets per team

Setup

- Prepare an outdoor course with 18 targets, e.g., the slide, the garbage can by the front doors, the fifth fence post on the west fence, the drinking fountain, the four-square court, the basketball hoop. Prepare a list of the targets for each team. Players will advance from one target to the next as they hit each target.

- Give each person a Frisbee and each group a list of the targets, and a piece of paper and pencil to use to keep score. Each player keeps his or her own score.
- Start each group at a different target so that everyone can be on the course at the same time.

Instructions

1. Players stand five paces away from the target. The first player in the group throws toward the target, then the next player, and so on until each player has thrown once toward the target.
2. Players then walk to their Frisbee and prepare to throw toward the target from the spot where the Frisbee landed. The player who is farthest from the target makes the first throw, then the next farthest makes the next throw, and so on.
3. Players record how many throws it takes them to hit the target.
4. After everyone in the group hits the target, the group moves to the next one and starts again.
5. After completing the course, the players add their scores and the lowest score wins.

Tips and Variations

- For player safety, players should not throw their Frisbee until the players in front of them are out of range.
- Frisbee Golf Race: Play the game as a race, without counting the number of throws. Instead, players simply hit all the targets as quickly as possible and record how long it takes to complete the course. The fastest time wins.

Ultimate

Objective

To score the most points as a team by catching the Frisbee over the opposing team's goal line

Players

Two teams of seven players

Equipment

One Frisbee

Setup

This game, also known as Ultimate Frisbee, should be played outside on a rectangular field slightly smaller than a soccer field, with a goal line at each end.

Instructions

1. The game begins with a "kickoff" in which one team throws the Frisbee across the field to the other team.
2. The offensive team can advance toward the other team's goal line by passing it to teammates. Defenders can knock the Frisbee to the ground or intercept a pass.
3. If the Frisbee is dropped, possession goes to the other team. They can pick up the Frisbee from where it is on the ground with no stop in play.
4. When a player has the Frisbee, she cannot run, but must look for a teammate to pass to.
5. Officially, a game lasts for two halves of 24 minutes each, but you can adjust the length to serve your needs.
6. Each time a player catches a Frisbee in the end zone, he scores a point.
7. The team with the most points at the end of the game is the winner.

Tips and Variations

- For complete rules go to the following Web site: www.ultimate-handbook.com/Webpages/Others/rules.html.
- Ultimate Tag: Players run with the Frisbee until they are tagged. When they are tagged, they must pass within three seconds.

Chapter 5

© Human Kinetics

Tag Games

Nearly everyone has fond memories of playing tag: the delight in running away from the player who is It, the agony in getting tagged, and for the It, the satisfaction of catching someone. Players run and run and run some more, without realizing all the exercise they are getting as they try to tag someone or as they try to avoid being tagged. Tag games are often great for warm-ups before other activities. Aside from the activity level that tag games encourage, the beauty of tag games is their simplicity. Typically, tag games require little or no equipment and can be organized in a moment's notice and are suitable for a handful of players or large groups. Most tag games work equally well in a gymnasium or outdoors.

General hint: For most tag games, don't allow touchbacks. A touchback is when a player is tagged and then tags back the player who just tagged him. Also, remind kids to be careful to tag, not push, the player they are chasing.

The games and illustrations in this chapter are adapted, by permission, from CIRA, *You're "It"! Tag, tag and more tag.* ©2001 CIRA Ontario.

Feet-Off-the-Ground Tag

Objectives

- For the Its to tag everyone, and for the others to avoid being tagged or to help those who have been tagged to reenter the game by picking up a tagged player
- To run, dodge, and tag

Players

Any number of players

Equipment

None

Setup

- Play this game in a gym or an outside area with players starting from scattered positions.
- Choose one or several Its.

Instructions

1. The Its try to tag free players.
2. Tagged players stand still with their arms at their sides. They can be freed only if a free player gives them a bear hug and lifts their feet off the ground.

Tips and Variations

Change Its regularly.

Racecar Tag

Objectives

- For the Its to tag everyone, and for the others to avoid being tagged or to help those tagged to reenter the game by fixing their flat tires
- To run, dodge, and tag

Players

Any number of players

Equipment

None

Setup

- Play this game in a gym or an outside area with players starting from scattered positions.
- Designate one or several Its.

Instructions

1. The players identified as racecars scatter, and the Its pursue them.

2. When an It tags a racecar, the racecar gets a flat tire and must kneel down on all fours with one elbow collapsed on the floor.

3. A fully running racecar can release the broken-down car by touching its head and saying "beep, beep." The disabled car slowly rises up as the flat tire inflates, says "varoom, varoom," and drives away.

Tips and Variations

None

Red Stop–Green Go Tag

Objectives

- For the Its to tag everyone
- For the others to avoid being tagged and for some players to help those tagged to reenter the game by giving them a green light
- To run, dodge, and tag

Players

Any number of players

Equipment

- Five red pinnies
- Five green pinnies

Setup

- Play this game in a gym or small outside area with players starting from scattered positions.
- Choose five players to wear red pinnies and to be the taggers.
- Choose five other players to wear green pinnies and to be the releasers.

Instructions

1. On the go signal, the red players try to tag the free players. If a red player touches a free player, the free player must stop.
2. A green player can touch a stopped player to free him.
3. Red players cannot tag green players.

Tips and Variations

Be sure all players have a chance to be red and to be green.

Bodyguard Tag

Objectives

- For the Its to tag the king while the bodyguards protect the king
- To run, dodge, and tag

Players

Groups of four to six players

Equipment

None

Setup

- Divide the players into groups of four to six, and assign each group a playing area.
- In each group designate a chaser and a king. The rest are body-guards.

Instructions

1. On the *go* signal, the chaser tries to tag the king.
2. The bodyguards, who move around with their hands on their hips, try to protect the king by keeping their bodies between the king and the chaser. Guards must stay at least one step away from the king.
3. A chaser cannot touch a guard because guards are ice cold and can freeze chasers. If a chaser comes in contact with a guard, the chaser must stand in a frozen position for five seconds before thawing and continuing to chase the king.
4. The chaser wins when she tags the king.

Tips and Variations

Change roles regularly to give all players the opportunity to play each role.

Bridge Tag

Objectives

For the Its to tag everyone, and for the others to avoid being tagged or to help those tagged to reenter the game by sliding under their bridge

Players

Any number of players

Equipment

None

Setup

- You can play this game in a gym or an outside area.
- Choose one or more Its.

Instructions

1. When an It tags a free player, the player must form a bridge by supporting herself on her hands and feet and lifting her body up.
2. To be released, a free player must go under the bridge.

Tips and Variations

- Have students create bridges both face up and face down.
- Change Its often, and increase the number of Its until they are able to catch all the free players.

Elbow Tag

Objectives

- For the Its to tag a player's elbow
- For the players to avoid being tagged

Players

Any number of players

Equipment

None

Setup

- Play this game in a gym or a similarly sized outside area.
- Choose three or four players to be It.
- Instruct the remaining players to pair up. Players face each other, and each player locks his left elbow with his partner's right elbow.

Instructions

1. On the *go* signal, the Its try to tag an elbow on any of the pairs.
2. When an It succeeds, she joins elbows with the player she tagged, and the partner of the tagged player becomes It.
3. There is no need to interrupt this game because the Its change regularly.

Tips and Variations

None

Toilet Tag

Objectives

- For the Its to tag everyone, and for the others to avoid being tagged and to help those who have been tagged to reenter the game by flushing the toilets
- To run, dodge, and tag

Players

Any number of players

Equipment

Three or four new toilet plungers or brushes

Setup

- Play this game in a gym or an equivalent outside area with players starting from scattered positions.
- Choose three or four players to be It, and give each one a toilet brush or plunger.

Instructions

1. On the *go* signal, the Its try to tag the other players with their hands.

2. If tagged, a player becomes a toilet by squatting down like a baseball catcher, one arm held straight out to the side (see figure on page 184).

3. In order for a tagged player to become free, a free player must push down the tagged players hand to "flush." After the toilet makes a flushing sound, the tagged player is free.

Tips and Variations

Change Its frequently.

Go Tag

Objectives

- For the chaser to tag the runner and the runner to avoid being tagged
- To run, dodge, tag, and solve problems

Players

Groups of 10 to 30 players

Equipment

None

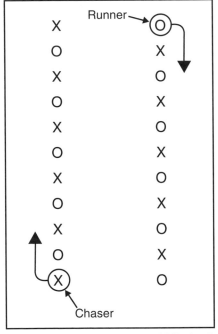

O Facing out   X Facing in

Setup

- The players squat in two long lines, with alternating players facing opposite directions—one player facing in and the next facing out.
- The player at one end of one line is the runner, and the player at the other end of the other line is the chaser.

Instructions

1. The chaser and runner begin running around the squatting players, the chaser trying to catch the runner. They can run in either direction and run outside of the group or between the two lines. They can change direction.
2. As the chaser runs around the squatting players, trying to catch the runner, she taps the back of any player and shouts "Go!" The tapped player becomes the chaser, while the old chaser squats in the new chaser's place in line. This maneuver, the go tag, enables the entire group to work together in the role of chaser.
3. Players cannot cut through the line of players.

Tips and Variations

The key is to change chasers frequently and catch the runner off guard. Speed is not as important as quick thinking. When the runner is finally tagged, she squats at the end of the line, and the player who tagged her becomes the new runner. The player at the other end of the line becomes the chaser.

Macarena Tag

Objectives

- For the Its to tag everyone, and for the others to avoid being tagged or to dance the Macarena to reenter the game
- To dance, run, dodge, and tag

Players

Any number of players

Equipment

- "Macarena" music
- Music player
- Two or three pinnies

Setup

- Play this game in a gym with players starting from scattered positions.
- Have the "Macarena" song playing.
- Designate two or three Its.

Instructions

1. On the signal to start, the Its try to tag free players.
2. When a player is tagged, he must stop and perform the entire sequence of the Macarena in order to free himself.
3. Because the dance repeats throughout the song, the tagged player must wait for the appropriate part of the song before starting the moves.

Tips and Variations

- Provide lots of time to teach the players the moves of the Macarena and allow them to practice before beginning.
- Macarena Tag nicely complements a dance lesson.
- Following are the moves for the dance:
  - Right hand goes out palm down.
  - Left hand goes out palm down.
  - Right palm up.
  - Left palm up.
  - Right hand to left shoulder.
  - Left hand to right shoulder.
  - Right hand to back of right ear.
  - Left hand to back of left ear.
  - Right hand to left hip.
  - Left hand to right hip.
  - Right hand to right buttock.
  - Left hand to left buttock.
  - Roll hips with hands on buttocks to the left.
  - Roll hips with hands on buttocks to the right.
  - Roll hips with hands on buttocks to the left.
  - Clap and return to the tag game.

Gator Tag

Objectives

- For the Its to tag everyone
- For the others to avoid being tagged
- To throw, catch, run, dodge, and tag

Players

Groups of 15 to 30 players

Equipment

- Three to six Gator balls
- Fifteen to thirty pinnies

Setup

- Play this game in a gym or equivalent outside area with players starting from scattered positions.
- Select two players to be It. Give each It a pinny, and give one of the Its a Gator ball.

Instructions

1. On the *go* signal, the Its may tag any free player by touching them with the ball.
2. This is not as easy as it sounds, because the taggers can pivot on one foot but cannot run with the ball. They will soon learn how to catch the ball, quickly pivot, and tag an unsuspecting player. When a free player is caught, he puts on a pinny and becomes a tagger.
3. As the number of Its increases, add more balls.
4. The game ends when all players have been tagged.

Tips and Variations

- Select Its who are good passers and catchers.
- Encourage teamwork and short passes to tag free players.
- If 25 to 30 people play, this game can take as long as 20 minutes.
- You may want to use an area smaller than an entire gym when you first play to keep the players close to each other.

Chapter 6

Hardware Store Games

Could your program benefit from renovation? Do you need to build an addition or two? What better place to start than your local hardware store, which contains possibilities for more than just home repair? Treat your local hardware store or home improvement store as an equipment room. Develop innovative and enjoyable games that use unexpected equipment. The options are limitless. Get players involved in creating their own games and teaching them to the group. Enjoy!

Unless otherwise noted, the games in this chapter are adapted, by permission, from CIRA, *Everything but the kitchen sink: Well maybe...* ©2005 CIRA Ontario. Photos on pages 191, 201, and 210 are reprinted, by permission, from CIRA, *Bang for your buck.* ©2004 CIRA Ontario.

TOILET PLUNGER GAMES

These fun and ridiculous pieces of equipment are a great addition to many games. Players can use them to propel themselves on scooters. The stronger the suction against the floor, the farther the players can propel themselves. But the real fun begins when the players must break the suction and lift the plunger. Plungers can also be used in place of pylons.

Pro Star Plumbers

Objective

To be the first team to pump all the plungers

Players

Groups of 5 to 10 players

Equipment

One toilet plunger per player

Setup

- Teams stand in a circle, with each player holding a toilet plunger and facing the inside of the circle.
- Number the handles of each plunger.

Instructions

1. Everyone pumps their toilet plunger two times on the floor in front of them, lifts their plunger, turns around to face out of the circle, pumps their plunger another two times, and then passes the plunger one to the left. The toilet plungers will sometimes get stuck to the floor, and players may have a hard time pulling their plunger off the floor and passing it to the next person.

2. Repeat this pattern until everyone is holding the toilet plunger they started with.

3. When each player on a team has his original plunger, players put their plungers into a tight circle, sit in a circle around the plungers with legs pointing out, and shout "flush!" The first team to flush wins.

Tips and Variations

None

Slalom Run

Objective

To quickly ski on scooters around pylons, using toilet plungers as poles

Players

Teams of three or four players

Equipment

- Two scooters per team
- Two toilet plungers per team
- Two pylons per team

Setup

- Set up identical, short slalom courses for the teams. For example, designate a starting line and place a pylon about three steps away from it and another pylon three steps from that.
- Teams line up and stand on the starting line in front of their pylon.

Instructions

1. Instruct the players how to position themselves on the scooter: sit or lie down. The first skier positions herself on two scooters and advances through the course by pushing herself forward with the two toilet plungers.
2. The skier makes a figure eight around the two pylons and crosses the start line. She gives the scooters and plungers to the next person in line and sits behind the starting line.
3. The next skier sits or lies on the scooters and pushes around the course.
4. The toilet plungers will sometimes get stuck, which makes it difficult to advance quickly and adds to the fun.
5. The first team to complete the course and return all members to the starting position is the winner.

Tips and Variations

- Safety tip: Warn students not to lean too far back when pushing so that they do not fall backward onto the floor.
- Tour de France Trip: Players ride tricycles, advancing with toilet plungers around the mountains (plastic trash cans) in the Tour de France.

© John Byl

Tank-Up Relay

Objectives

- To be the first team to stack plastic pipe on a plunger
- To develop logic and problem-solving skills

Players

Teams of three or four players

Equipment

- Two scooters per team
- Three toilet plungers per team
- Nine pieces of plastic pipe per team, 1.5 to 2 inches wide; three each at lengths of 1, 3.5, and 6 inches (2, 9, and 15 cm)

Setup

- Designate a starting line for each team, and line up each team behind it with a scooter and two plungers.
- Place a toilet plunger immediately in front of each team.
- Place the three short pieces of pipe two paces past the starting line, place the three medium pieces of pipe two paces beyond that, and place the three long pieces of pipe two paces beyond that.

Instructions

1. On the *go* signal, the first team member sits on the scooter and propels himself with the plungers to a pile of plastic pipe. He grabs a piece and hurries back to the team. After he slides the pipe over the handle of the toilet plunger, the next person can go.

2. Teams will have to decide on a strategy to fill their handle the quickest. Shorter pieces are closer to the team and can be gathered quickly. But the longer pieces of pipe that are farther away and take time to gather will fill more space on the handle, so they may be the best choice.

3. End the relay after a minute. The team that stacks the pipe highest on the handle wins.

Tips and Variations

Fill 'Er Up: Play the game the same way, but the first team to stack the pieces of pipe higher than the top of the plunger handle wins.

CARPET GAMES

Squares of carpet, flipped up or down, can make games more interesting by providing a different way of moving! Walking with carpet squares under the feet is a great equalizer, especially in games like basketball and floor hockey. Choosing bright colors makes using carpet squares even more appealing to students.

Carpet Shoe Sports

Objective

To compete in sports on a more equal, safe, and strenuous level by having all players shuffle around the playing area on pieces of carpet

Players

Teams of five to eight players

Equipment

- Two carpet "shoes" per player
- Balls, goals, and other sport-specific equipment as needed

Setup

- The setup depends on the sport, but typically you will need to establish a goal or goal line and assign players to their sides.
- Give each player two carpet pieces to use as carpet shoes.

Instructions

Turn a gymnasium into an "ice rink" and have players "skate" on carpet shoes. Players can play floor hockey, football, and basketball on carpet shoes.

Tips and Variations

Safety tip: Give players the opportunity to practice moving around on their shoes before starting an organized activity.

Indoor Game Boards

Objective

To complete the quiet, low-activity-level, problem-solving game first

Players

Two players play each game; for some games other players can act as game pieces.

Equipment

- Enough carpet squares for the game chosen (9 for tic-tac-toe, 64 for checkers, 42 for Connect Four)
- Up to 42 pinnies or pieces of construction paper in two different colors (5 each for tic-tac-toe, 12 each for checkers, and 21 each for Connect Four)
- Twenty-four beanbags in two different colors

Setup

Lay out carpet squares to create life-size game boards: tic-tac-toe (3 × 3), Connect Four (7 × 6), or checkers (8 × 8).

Instructions

1. The students play these traditional games on the large game boards.
2. For tic-tac-toe, the players can be the pieces, but for Connect Four and checkers, it may be better to use colored beanbags because these games take much longer.

Tips and Variations

Modify other games into life-size versions.

Chivalry Competition

Objective

To race against other nobles to see who can cross the playing area the fastest

Players

Any number of pairs

Equipment

One carpet square per player

Setup

- Establish a starting line and a finish line.
- Players stand with their partner behind the starting line. One of the partners holds two carpet squares.

Instructions

1. The "lady" must cross the playing area by stepping only on the carpet squares laid out by the "lord." The lord may step anywhere in the playing area.
2. On the go signal, the lord lays the two carpet squares on the ground.
3. As soon as the lady steps from the back square onto the front square, the lord moves the back square to the front.

Tips and Variations

Swamp Crossing: Create teams of 5-10 players and distribute one square per two people. In this version everyone on the team must cross the playing area by stepping only on carpet squares. The team lays out the squares and moves forward until they get to the end of their supply. Then the team tries to fit onto as few squares as possible, so that they can pass the carpets from the back forward.

ROPE GAMES

Ropes: They can be skipped, shaped, wrapped, tugged, lassoed, and more! Soft, hand-friendly ropes are perfect physical education tools. Heavier ropes make super skipping ropes. For many of these games, you can use elastics tied together instead of rope.

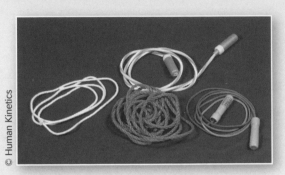

© Human Kinetics

Shapes in the Dark

Objective

To form a designated shape as a blindfolded team

Players

Even teams of three to nine players

Equipment

- One long rope for each team
- One blindfold for each player

Setup

- Players stand in a group, all holding onto a rope.
- Ensure that every player is properly blindfolded.
- Assign a shape (e.g., a triangle). Increase the complexity of the shape as the players get better at the game.

Instructions

1. On the signal to begin, the group tries to form the designated shape. Every member must remain in contact with the rope.

2. When the team feels they have accomplished the task, they remove the blindfold and observe their results.

Tips and Variations

- Safety tip: Stay with their group so they do not walk into things.
- Safety tip: Instruct the players to move slowly.
- Shape Race: Establish a time limit and see which team is closest when the time is up.
- Inside Out: Everyone gets inside the shape instead of standing outside of it. Or, alternate and have half of the players stand inside the rope while half stand outside of it.

Adapted, by permission, from CIRA, *Bang for your buck.* ©2004 CIRA Ontario.

Woven-Together Web

Objective

To learn each other's names

Players

Groups of 10 to 15 players

Equipment

One ball of string

Setup

- Players stand in a circle with approximately one step between them and the player on either side of them.
- Give one of the players a ball of string.

Instructions

1. The first player starts by holding an end of the string with one hand and tossing the ball of string with the other while saying the name of the person she is passing it to.
2. Once everyone holds a piece of the string, players toss the ball around again, this time to new people.
3. The new friends have created a web!
4. Now reverse the process; the players roll the string back into a ball, saying the name of the person they are passing to.

Tips and Variations

- This is a great game to play on the first day of the school year or any time people first meet.
- Crossing the Web: When the web is complete, call several players names. They drop their holds, duck under the web, and then take over someone else's hold. Do this several times before reversing the process (players learn even more names this way).

Froggy Fall Over

Objective

To pull your opponent off balance

Players

Any number of pairs

Equipment

One soft rope (1 yard [1 m] long) per pair

Setup

Two players hold opposite ends of a rope while in a squatting position.

Instructions

1. Each player tries to tip his opponent off balance by pulling on the rope.
2. A player wins when the other player lets go of the rope, loses balance, moves a foot, touches the ground with his hand, or falls over.

Tips and Variations

- Safety tip: Because players are in a squatting position, it's unlikely they'll hurt themselves when they lose their balance. However, playing this game on a wrestling mat is safest.
- Hold a minitournament. The winner of the first round competes with another winner, while the loser challenges another loser. Go through this process several times until only two players have won all their competitions. The winner of the final challenge is the overall winner.
- Stork Stand: Players stand on one foot, hold onto a rope, and try to pull each other off balance.

Careful, Minefield

Objectives

- To pick up a Frisbee without stepping into the circle
- To develop problem-solving and cooperation skills

Players

Groups of four to six players

Equipment

- One rope 6 to 11 yards (6-11 m) long
- One Frisbee per team
- Several gymnastics mats

Setup

- Create a "minefield" by making a circle out of the rope on top of the gymnastics mats.
- The Frisbee (or other piece of equipment) is the bomb in the center of the minefield.
- The circle must be large enough that a player cannot just reach into the circle and grab the bomb (Frisbee) without assistance.

Instructions

1. Players must get the bomb out of the minefield without dragging it or stepping inside the bounds of the minefield.
2. The main method for solving this problem requires players to hold each other as one person braces to pick up the mine.

Tips and Variations

Minefield With Assistance. Consider adding a couple of pieces of strong rope or a pole to help the group.

WOOD GAMES

Aspiring lumberjacks and carpenters will love trying out these fun games. You can use these games in a series of career-related theme games. Students learn basic life skills while completing challenges and having fun!

Beam Balance Challenge

Objectives

To explore different ways of crossing various beams and to demonstrate balance

Players

Any number of players

Equipment

- Several 2 × 4s (40 × 90 mm) and planks of various sizes
- Chairs (optional)

Setup

Set up an obstacle course. You could include a low balance beam (a 2 × 4 that players may not step off of), a short path of connected planks, a "hurdle" to step over, and a tunnel to crawl through formed by 2 × 4s supported between two chairs.

Instructions

1. Players explore different ways through the obstacle course.
2. Players develop an artistic routine across the obstacle course, either singly or in pairs. Either the leader or the other participants score the routine; 10 is the maximum score. The individual or pair with the highest score is the winner.

Tips and Variations

- Make sure the wood is sturdy and free of splinters.
- Emphasize to the players that they must travel across the course in a safe manner.
- Look Into My Eyes: Two players walk through the course facing each other, supporting a soft object such as a balloon or Gator ball between their heads.
- Waiter Training: A player balances a tray on her shoulder, holding it with one hand as she goes through the course.

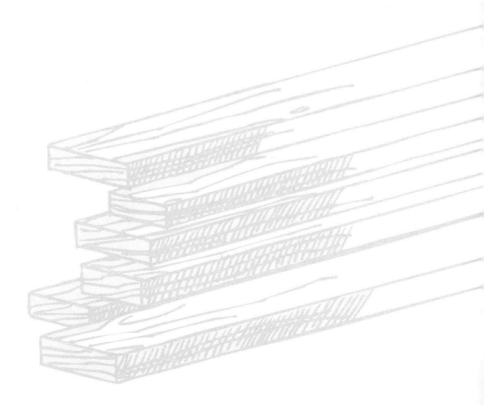

Switch-er-roo!

Objectives

- To reverse the order of a line of players standing on a board in the quickest time, without stepping on the ground
- To develop problem-solving and team-building skills

Players

Groups of 5 to 10 players

Equipment

Two 2 × 4 (40 × 90 mm) boards per team that are long enough for the whole team to stand on; the length should be one yard (1 meter) per every three people

Setup

- Lay out two boards side by side with a small gap between them for each team.
- Each team stands on their boards in a single file line. Each player has one foot on each board.

Instructions

1. On the signal to start, players begin reversing the order of their line.
2. Players may not step on the floor. Each time a player touches the floor, the leader adds five seconds to the team's time, so players must be careful to stay on the boards.
3. Groups try to complete the task as quickly as possible and try to improve their time in subsequent tries.

Tips and Variations

Team vs. Team Switch-er-roo: Instead of competing against time, each team competes against the other teams. If a player touches the ground, all the players on that team must return to their original position before trying again.

Architect

Objective

To create the highest stack within the time limit

Players

Teams of three to five players

Equipment

Thirty wood blocks of various shapes and sizes per team

Setup

Assign each group a spot and give them approximately 30 pieces of wood each.

Instructions

Give teams two minutes to build the highest freestanding structure they can with the blocks they have.

Tips and Variations

Design Architects: Players create a specific shape such as a boat, a person, or a dog within the time limit.

BINS AND BALLS

Trash bins are not just for garbage. They can also be used as targets for Gator balls and beanbags, large obstacles to avoid, primitive drums, and places to hide surprises.

© Human Kinetics

Bucketball

Objective

To score more buckets than your opponent

Players

Two teams of five to seven players each

Equipment

- Two bins or buckets
- One basketball or Gator ball

Setup

- Set up a court similar to a basketball court. Instead of using two basketball hoops, set up two scoring areas where a player with a bucket will stand, such as in the basketball court key or in a hula hoop.
- Divide the players into two teams.
- Each team designates a "catcher," who holds a bucket and stands in the designated area.

Instructions

1. Begin the game with a jump ball at center court.
2. The teams dribble and pass the ball to advance toward their catcher.
3. Only the catchers may enter the basketball keys.
4. When a player is close enough to the catcher, he passes the ball to the catcher, who must catch it in the bucket.
5. A successful catch results in a point, and the team scored on gains possession of the ball.

Tips and Variations

- Four-Corner Bucketball: Play with four teams and more balls.
- Passing Bucketball: Play the same way, but the player with the ball may not move. This emphasizes good passing and shooting and makes noncontact defense much easier to enforce.

Adapted, by permission, from CIRA, *Bang for your buck.* ©2004 CIRA Ontario.

Movement Memory

Objective

To uncover sports equipment and claim matching pieces by remembering their locations

Players

Two teams of three to five players

Equipment

- Twenty small or large plastic trash cans
- Ten assorted pairs of matching equipment

Setup

- Set up a big "memory board" in the playing area by arranging the trash cans in a four-by-five grid.
- Put one piece of physical education equipment, e.g., skipping rope, plastic disk, pylon, rubber chicken, sport ball, Gator ball, tee-ball stand, under each trash can. Don't let the players see where you put the equipment.
- Divide the group into two teams.

Instructions

1. Teams gather around the memory board, and all players lightly jog on the spot. One team at a time lifts two trash cans to try to uncover matching equipment, for example, both basketballs.
2. If the team uncovers a match, the whole team does 10 jumping jacks and gives each other high fives. They also get to try to make another match, and they set the equipment aside so they can count it up at the end of the game.
3. If the team does not make a match, they choose a quick activity for the whole group to perform. It may help to have ideas on hand (e.g., everyone does 10 sit-ups, runs around the gym once, crab walks around a badminton court).
4. The team with the most matches wins.

Tips and Variations

Activity Memory: Place pieces of paper under the bins with instructions for certain activities. You can also place related equipment under the bins. The team performs the activities under the bins they chose. If they make a match they pull out their activity sheets so they can count them at the end of the game.

Garbage Can Target Toss

Objective

To be the team that tosses the most items into a trash can

Players

Teams of three or four players

Equipment

- One trash can per team
- Six to ten pieces of small, tossable equipment (e.g., beanbags, Hacky Sacks, Frisbees, Gator balls) per team

Setup

- Designate a restraining line and line up each team behind it.
- Place a trash can in front of each team five paces away from the line.
- Only the first player has a piece of equipment and the rest of the items should be piled next to the team.

Instructions

1. On the *go* signal, the first player tosses her piece of equipment into the trash can.
2. If she misses, she does five jumping jacks, picks up the missed item, and gives it to the next player to try.
3. Players take turns throwing equipment into their trash can.
4. After a specified time, the team with the most objects in the trash can wins.

Tips and Variations

Toss and Exercise: Players toss their beanbags into bins full of cards with different exercises on them. When a player scores, he gets a card, and the whole team does the activity specified on the card.

Waddle-Walk Chin-Duck

Objective

To transfer a ball from one garbage can to another more times than the other teams do

Players

Teams of three or four players

Equipment

- Two small trash cans per team
- One table tennis or Gator ball per team

Setup

- Designate a playing area for each team by setting up their two garbage cans 10 steps apart.
- Place the ball in one of the cans, and position the team behind that can.

Instructions

1. This game is a relay in which players take turns moving their ball from one can to the other by carrying one ball under their chin or between their knees.
2. On the *go* signal, the first runner picks up the ball and places it either under her chin or between her knees and carries it to the far garbage can. She drops it in the can and returns to the starting can. Once she returns, the next player gets the ball and transfers it to the other can.
3. Each team counts out loud the number of times they transfer the ball from one garbage can to the other.
4. After a specified period of play, the team that transferred the ball the most times is the winner.

Tips and Variations

Combined Challenge: Players carry two balls at the same time: one under the chin and one between their knees!

NUTS AND BOLTS GAMES

With a handful of nuts, an extra-large bolt, and an oversized imagination, you can create many unconventional games. For the following two games, the nuts and bolts are treasures.

Mechanical Tag

Objective

For the tagger to tag everyone before all the nuts are found and placed on the bolts

Players

At least 20 players

Equipment

- Four bolts per 20 players (one for each bolter)
- One nut per player
- One pinny per 20 players

Setup

- Hide nuts around the playing area. Some suggested hiding spots are corners of the gym, on a door handle or a light switch, etc.
- Designate one tagger for approximately every 20 players. The tagger wears a pinny.
- Designate four bolters for approximately every 20 players, and give each bolter a bolt.
- Everyone else is a seeker.

Instructions

1. On the *go* signal, seekers look for nuts within the playing area and taggers try to tag seekers.
2. When a seeker finds a nut, she puts her hands above her head and spins in a circle to alert the bolters that she's found a nut.

3. The bolters are the only players who can pick up a nut. When someone finds a nut, a bolter runs over, picks up the nut, and puts it on his bolt. Bolters cannot be tagged.

4. As seekers search for the nuts, they must be careful to stay away from the taggers. The taggers try to tag all the seekers before the bolters get all of the nuts.

5. When a seeker is tagged, she must slowly jog in a small circle until the bolters have all the nuts or until all the seekers have been tagged.

Tips and Variations

Safety tip: Players may not throw the nuts. Seekers may only signal the location of a bolt to a bolter by spinning.

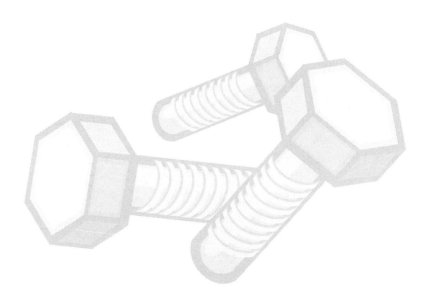

Tolkien Tag

Objective

To recover as much treasure as possible and escape within the time limit

Players

Ten to thirty players

Equipment

- Eighteen gold-colored nuts
- Three hula hoops
- One yellow pinny
- Three green pinnies
- Tape

Setup

- Scatter the three hula hoops around the gym on intersecting lines.
- Set up three jewel stockpiles by placing six nuts inside each hoop.
- Designate three players to be Smaug the dragon, who owns the jewels. Each Smaug wears a green pinny and stands by the jewels.
- The rest of the players are in a scattered formation but on lines in the playing area.
- Place the yellow pinny inside one of the hoops. This pinny represents the ring.
- Designate an area of the gym as the pit (a place where tagged players must go to perform a task before rejoining the game).
- Designate a corner of the gym as the cave exit.

Instructions

1. During the game, adventurers (players) try to obtain all of the jewels from the stockpiles and then escape from the cave. Adventurers may take three jewels at a time. The dragons try to tag the adventurers. When tagged, the adventurers must return jewels in their possession and go to the pit.

2. On the *go* signal, players walk through the passageways in the mountain cave (the lines on the gym floor) toward the jewels. Players may not skip over lines. (You may need to add a few more lines with tape, especially around the treasure piles.)

3. When an adventurer is wearing the ring (the yellow pinny), he is invisible and Smaug cannot tag him. Therefore, dragons must prioritize how to guard the area, because "Bilbo Baggins" can quickly remove the rest of the jewels when wearing the ring. The adventurers will need to strategize how to get the ring (yellow pinny) from the hoop.

4. When a dragon tags an adventurer, she goes into the pit and must climb out before rejoining the game. Players can "climb out" by performing an activity such as jogging in place for one minute or skipping 60 times.

Tips and Variations

None

TARP GAMES

Tarps are not just for hanging overhead; they also make excellent volleyball nets, parachutes, and life-size game boards. The possibilities are limitless.

Keep It Rolling

Objective

To roll a ball around a tarp as many times as possible

Players

Groups of 4 to 10 players

Equipment

- One tarp
- One Gator ball or other soft ball per group

Setup

- Players stand around a tarp and hold it at waist level.
- Place a ball on the tarp near one edge.

Instructions

1. On the *go* signal, the players move the tarp so that the ball rolls around it.
2. The ball must move at all times, so players do not want to cradle it in the middle. Cut a ball-size hole in the middle of the tarp to encourage students to keep the ball rolling away from the middle.
3. The team counts how many times the ball circles the tarp before falling off.

Tips and Variations

- Play other favorite parachute games with the more awkward tarps.
- Tarp to Tarp: Use two tarps per team. Place the ball on one tarp held by half the team. The other half of the team carries its tarp past the other tarp by going around it, going over it, going under it, or going any other way the team can think of. The half-team with the ball passes the ball onto the empty tarp and then goes ahead of the other half-team to receive the ball. Have teams pass the ball the length of a gym or half the length of a soccer field.

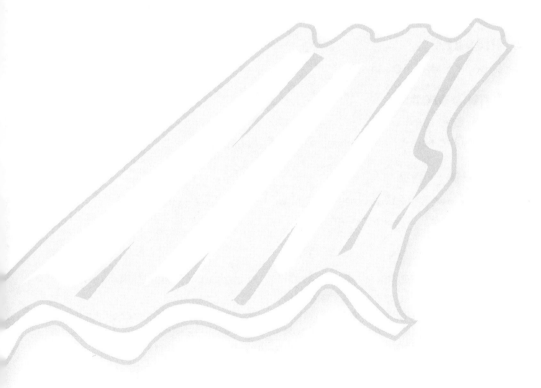

Ocean Hazards

Objective

To avoid being eaten by a shark

Players

Eight to fifteen players

Equipment

One large blue tarp

Setup

- Players lie on a slippery floor, holding the tarp. Their legs and waist are under a tarp.
- Designate one player to be the shark. The shark starts under the tarp.
- Designate one player be the lifeguard and stand outside of the tarp near the players.

Instructions

1. On the *go* signal, the players move the tarp up and down in a wave pattern. When the water is wavy, the shark grabs an unsuspecting swimmer by the legs and pulls him under the water. The shark trades places with the swimmer, and the swimmer becomes the shark.
2. When a swimmer feels the pull from the shark, he can call to the lifeguard to pull him in the opposite direction and help him keep from being pulled under the water.

Tips and Variations

No Swimmers Left: Victims do not trade places with the sharks, but become sharks themselves. Play until there are not enough people left to hold up the tarp.

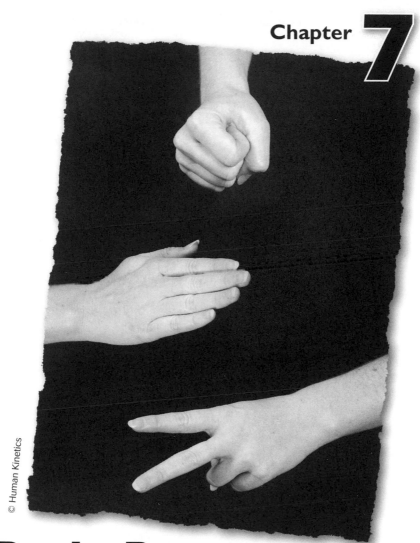

Chapter 7

© Human Kinetics

Rock, Paper, Scissors Games

Rock, paper, scissors games have been around for a long time. We've taken the basic game of rock, paper, scissors and generated variations requiring lots of fun physical activity.

During the traditional rock, paper, scissors procedure, called a *throw*, competitors say go, then count out "one, two" while displaying a fist in front of them, and then on "three," displaying paper or rock or scissors.

Paper is represented by a flat hand, rock by a fist, and scissors by two fingers. A variation of this three-count throw is quick draw. In quick draw competitors place their throwing hand in their armpit. They say, "ready, go," and pull out their hand to display paper, rock, or scissors.

To determine the winner of rock, paper, scissors, use the following guidelines:

- Paper covers a rock.
- Rock smashes scissors.
- Scissors cut paper.

If there is a tie, play the game again.

Using rock, paper, scissors in a game format is a lot of fun. You can also use it to solve all kinds of conflicts when two or more people want the same thing—a quick game should resolve the conflict quickly. For more information, take a look at the Web site for the World Rock, Paper, Scissors Society: www.worldrps.com.

The games in this chapter are adapted, by permission, from CIRA, *Why paper & scissors rock!!!* ©2003 CIRA Ontario. Unless otherwise noted, the photos in this chapter are reprinted, by permission, from CIRA, *Why paper & scissors rock!!!* ©2003 CIRA Ontario.

Ha Ha

Objective

To have a player's partner run

Players

Any number of pairs

Equipment

None

Setup

- Designate a starting line and a target line 10 to 20 paces away.
- Players line up in pairs on the starting line.

Instructions

1. Partners face each other and play rock, paper, scissors.
2. The loser runs to the target line and back. When he returns, the partners play again and the loser runs.

Tips and Variations

- Play this as a warm-up activity.
- Ha Ha Exercise: Instead of running, players do an exercise such as 5 push-ups or 10 sit-ups.
- No-Wait Ha Ha: When a partner wins, the winner selects another partner who is standing at the starting line and they play rock, paper, scissors. This keeps more people active because players do not have to stand at the line waiting for their partner to complete the run or exercise.

Quick-Draw Four Square

Objectives

To get to square number one, or the king's square, and stay there

Players

Four to seven players per game

Equipment

None

Setup

- Set up a four-square box and use established four-square rotations, with the king in square 1 and three other players in squares 2, 3, and 4.
- One player stands in each of the four squares. The rest of the players line up outside of square four. Players in the squares tuck their hands in their armpits.

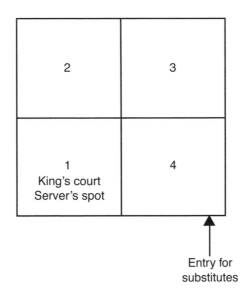

Instructions

1. The leader or king (player in square one) calls the name of one of the players in square two, three, or four, and the king plays quick-draw rock, paper, scissors with that person.
2. If the king wins, she stays in her spot and challenges another player. The loser goes to the end of the line and everybody moves up one square.
3. If the king loses, she moves to the end of the line and everyone moves up one square.
4. If a player throws a signal when his name hasn't been called, he moves to the end of the line.
5. Have players jog in place when they are in one of the squares.

Tips and Variations

When players are waiting their turn, they jog around the outside of the four-square.

Team Baseball

Objective

To score the most runs as a team

Players

Two teams of 6 to 12 players

Equipment

Four markers for bases (pylons work well)

Setup

- Set up a half-sized baseball diamond.
- Separate the group into two teams.
- Team A lines up behind and to the right of home base; team B lines up behind and to the left of home base.
- The first player from team A gets set to run around the bases in a clockwise fashion.
- The first player from team B gets set to run around the bases in a counterclockwise fashion.

Instructions

1. On the *go* signal, the first person from team A runs toward third base, and the first person from team B runs toward first base. They continue around the diamond toward second base.

2. When the runners meet, they play rock, paper, scissors. The winner continues around the diamond while the other player goes to the center of the diamond, does 10 jumping jacks, and then returns to the end of his line.

3. The next person in the line from the team that lost the rock, paper, scissors game, runs out to meet the approaching winner. When they meet (probably at first or third base) they play rock, paper, scissors. Each winner continues to advance around the diamond. If the same player wins, she will probably meet her next opponent halfway between first or third base and home.

4. The winner of the rock, paper, scissors challenge raises his hand so the teams know when to send their next player. Winners could

also identify themselves by carrying a rubber chicken or other object as they run.

5. Continue to play and count a run when a person crosses home plate. When someone crosses home plate, two players start the game again. After a specified time, end the game, and the team with the most runs is the winner.

Tips and Variations

Wacky Noodle Rock, Paper, Scissors Baseball: One runner carries a pool noodle. The one who wins gets the pool noodle. This makes it easier for the next runner to know who won. The winner can whack the loser. If the winner wins three rounds in a row and whacks all three people, he scores a run and the next person goes.

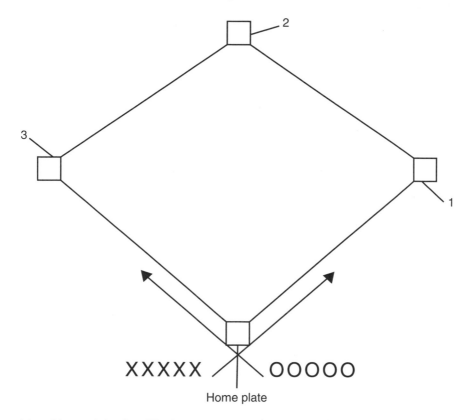

Home plate

Adapted, by permission, from CIRA, *Why paper & scissors rock!!!* ©2003 CIRA Ontario.

Evolution

Objective

To try to become Super Bird

Players

A group of 10 to 50 players

Equipment

None

Setup

Players squat in a scattered formation in the playing area.

Instructions

1. Players all start the game acting like an egg and waddling low to the ground.
2. Players waddle around until they meet someone to play rock, paper, scissors with. Winners evolve into a chicken and stay low to the ground, clucking and flapping their wings. Losers remain eggs.
3. Everyone keeps playing. Chickens who win evolve into dinosaurs and stand and clap their arms in front of them, simulating a large mouth. Chickens who lose must regress to eggs.
4. Finally, if players win as dinosaurs, they evolve into supreme beings who get to walk around and high five other supreme beings.
5. Eggs can only play eggs, chickens play chickens, and so on. Encourage players not to use words, but to make appropriate noises for their characters.
6. If a player loses a match, she regresses one stage. Eggs, of course, cannot regress.

Tips and Variations

Cooperative Evolution: Players do not regress in this game. When a player becomes a supreme being, she can help other players evolve to the next level. If the supreme being wins nothing happens to her, but if the supreme being loses, her partner moves up one level. It is more efficient if players stay with one player until he or she evolves. When both players have become supreme beings, they move on to other players. The goal is to evolve the group into supreme beings within the set time limit.

Reprinted, by permission, from CIRA, *Why paper & scissors rock!!!* ©2003 CIRA Ontario.

Versus the Leader

Objective

To beat the leader

Players

A large group of players

Equipment

None

Setup

- The leader stands at one side of the playing area, visible to everyone in the group.
- The group scatters themselves throughout the playing area, facing the leader.

Instructions

1. The leader and players all jump three times. On the third jump, the players deliver their rock, paper, scissors throw. The leader jumps a fourth time and delivers her throw.
   - For paper, stand with hands outstretched.
   - For scissors, stand with hands crossed over chest.
   - For rock, squat.
2. Depending on the outcome of the throw, players perform a certain physical activity, specified by the leader.
   - If players beat the leader, they high-five who did too.
   - If players tie the leader, they do half of the physical activity.
   - If players lose to the leader, they do the entire physical activity.

Tips and Variations

Everyone's a Leader: When a player loses he joins the leader. All the leaders decide together what they will throw. Play until only one person is left. That player is the winner.

Reentry Tag

Objective

To stay in or return to a game of tag

Players

Any number of players

Equipment

None

Setup

Set up the playing area and designate a player to be It according to the requirements of the particular tag game the group will play.

Instructions

1. On the *go* signal, players begin a tag game in a small, defined area.
2. When a player is tagged, he goes outside the boundaries of the playing area, finds another person who is out, and plays a game of rock, paper, scissors.
3. The winner of the rock, paper, scissors contest reenters the game. The loser moves on to challenge another player.

Tips and Variations

None

Second-Chance Tag

Objective

To avoid being tagged

Players

The number of players suitable for a specific tag game

Equipment

None

Setup

Set up the playing area and designate a player to be It according to the requirements of the particular tag game the group will play.

Instructions

1. On the *go* signal, players begin playing tag.
2. When It tags a player, the two play a game of rock, paper, scissors.
3. If It wins, the tagged player is It. If It loses, It must try to tag a different player.

Tips and Variations

None

One-Down Football

Objective

To win possession of the football by playing rock, paper, scissors

Players

Two teams of five to seven players

Equipment

One football

Setup

- Set up a small football field.
- Each team starts on its own half. One team starts with the ball at the center of a small football field, ready to kick off to the other team.

Instructions

1. Players use standard football rules, except that a team plays just one down.
2. Following the down, one player from each team takes part in a rock, paper, scissors contest. The team that wins the rock, paper, scissors throw gets the ball for the next down.

Tips and Variations

Rock, Paper, Scissors Basketball: Play regular basketball, but after a player scores a basket, a player from each team plays rock, paper, scissors. If the shooting team wins, the basket counts; if the losing team wins, the basket does not count.

Stand Alone

Objective

To avoid standing alone

Players

Groups of 7, 9, or 11 players

Equipment

One chair per person (minus one for the person standing in the middle)

Setup

- Arrange pairs of chairs facing each other in a circle.
- One player stands alone in the middle of the circle.
- The other players sit in the chairs.

Instructions

1. Seated players play rock, paper, scissors with the person facing them. The losers must move to another chair.
2. When a chair becomes vacant, the person in the middle tries to get to it before someone else switching chairs reaches it.
3. The person who does not get a chair stands alone in the middle until another chair opens.

Tips and Variations

None

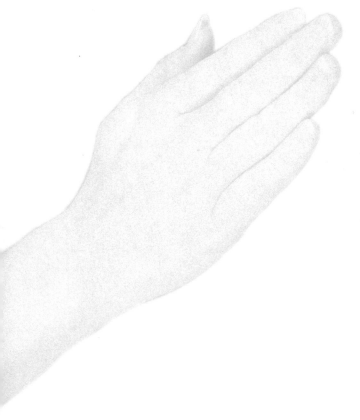

Train

Objective

To try to end up as the engine of a train made up of all the players

Players

Any number of players

Equipment

None

Setup

Players are scattered throughout the playing area.

Instructions

1. Players find someone to play rock, paper, scissors with. The losing player stands behind the winning player, holding her waist.

2. The player in front finds another pair to play and competes with the front person in that pair. The loser in that competition joins the end of the train.

3. The group continues playing and joining trains until two trains play each other in a final competition.

4. When the entire group forms one train, start again, or move to a desired location with the players all in one line.

Tips and Variations

- This is a great classroom activity when a teacher wants a line of students to walk somewhere.

- Train Huddle: Play this game like Train, but the entire train huddles and decides what to throw (rock, paper, scissors). When both teams are ready, both teams jump in the air once, twice, and then make their throw.

Race to Five

Objective

To collect five points as quickly as possible

Players

Groups of about five players

Equipment

None

Setup

Members of each group sit in a circle facing the other players in their group.

Instructions

1. The group counts one, two, then throws rock, paper, scissors. Each player looks at the person on either side and determines if he won or lost against each of these people.
2. Players score plus one point for each win, negative one point for each loss, and nothing for a tie.
3. Players keep track of the score with the fingers of the nonthrowing hand. Fingers pointing up indicate a positive score, fingers pointing down a negative score.
4. When someone reaches five points, restart the game after mixing up the groups. (The winner can move to another group.)
5. A person cannot score lower than negative-five points.

Tips and Variation

Mass Total to Five: Play this game the same way, except that players compete against the entire group—adding a point for everyone they beat and subtracting a point for everyone they lose to. The first person to five points or more is the winner. If there is a tie, the winners play a game of rock, paper, scissors to break the tie.

Pennies

Objective

To collect as many pennies as possible in 3 minutes

Players

Any number of players

Equipment

Two hundred pennies

Setup

- Players start in scattered positions around the playing area.
- Give each player three pennies.
- One or more leaders spread out in the playing area and hold the extra pennies.

Instructions

1. Players challenge each other to a rock, paper, scissors game. If a player wins, he gets his opponent's penny.
2. Players continue to challenge other players to collect as many pennies as possible.
3. Players who are out of pennies can challenge the leaders for more pennies to get back into the game.

Tips and Variations

None

Active Push 'Em Back

Objective

To be the first player to step back the designated number of steps

Players

Any number of pairs

Equipment

None

Setup

Pairs line up facing each other, creating two lines down the middle of the playing area.

Instructions

1. Each pair plays a series of rock, paper, scissors games.
2. Each time a player wins, she takes a step back. The loser stays in place.
3. Players play again.
4. Players win by taking a designated number of steps back or reaching the end of a designated playing area, e.g., the gym wall.

Tips and Variations

Players jog on the spot as they make their throws and take a step back.

About the Authors

John Byl, PhD, is a professor of physical education at Redeemer University College in Ancaster, Ontario, Canada, where he teaches courses in elementary health and physical education. He has directed high school and college intramurals for more than 30 years and has coached a variety of sports at the community, high school, and college levels. He also has served as an advisor on league and tournament formats for amateur and professional leagues.

Byl has authored and coauthored several books, including *101 Fun Warm-Up and Cool-Down Games, Intramural Recreation: Step-by-Step Guide to Creating an Effective Program, Co-Ed Recreational Games,* and *Organizing Successful Tournaments.* He serves as the president of CIRA (Canadian Intramural Recreation Association) Ontario and vice president of Sport Hamilton. Byl earned his PhD in organization, administration and policy from State University of New York at Buffalo, a master's degree in human kinetics from the University of Windsor, and a bachelor's degree in physical education from the University of British Columbia.

Herwig Baldauf recently retired as the head of physical and health education at Niagara District Secondary School, Niagara-on-the-Lake, Ontario, where he taught for 28 years. In that time Baldauf served on the executive boards of CIRA Ontario, CAHPERD, and Ophea (Ontario Physical and Health Education Association). He has published several resources for CIRA Ontario and Ophea and is coeditor of CAHPERD's *The Clipboard* series. Baldauf is a regular workshop presenter and has done numerous presentations at a variety of provincial and national conferences and has taught at the University of Toronto and Brock University in St. Catharines, Ontario.

Baldauf has been described as a visionary with progressive and innovative ideas and has been recognized with awards from his peers in the teaching profession, including the Ontario Secondary School Teacher's Federation Excellence in Education Award.

Pat Doyle is a retired elementary school physical education teacher who now operates Creative Playgrounds, a business that designs playgrounds and games. Since 2002 he has given more than 200 Active Playground workshops across Canada to promote physical activity for children on playgrounds.

Doyle was president of the Canadian Intramural Recreation Association of Ontario for six years and has authored or coauthored nine games resources and the Human Kinetics–produced *Game On.* He received a BA from the University of Windsor and a BA in education from the University of Western Ontario. He resides in Kitchener, Ontario.

Andy Raithby, MA, has taught in elementary schools of Ontario for more than 20 years, the last 11 as the head of physical education and health at Lisgar Middle School in Mississauga. His school has been the recipient of six Outstanding Intramural Achievement Awards. He has been an executive member of CIRA Ontario since 1996. Andy has coauthored several books with other CIRA members and is the sole author of *The World's Greatest Dodgeball Games*, *Great Games by Great Kids*, and the upcoming *Basketball 101*. He has presented across the country as an executive member of CIRA Ontario. His workshops have been described as motivating, inspiring, and, best of all, a lot of fun.

Andy is currently a course manager at the Ontario Educational Leadership Centre in Orillia, Ontario. He lives in Burlington, Ontario, with his wife and two great kids. When he's not doing CIRA "stuff" he's on his mountain bike, regularly cycling over 3,000 kilometers a year.

About CIRA Ontario

CIRA Ontario's mission is to encourage, promote, and develop active living, healthy lifestyles, and personal growth through intramural and recreational programs. CIRA Ontario believes that everyone should have the opportunity to participate in athletic and recreational activities, regardless of skill or fitness level, and that a well-constructed intramural and recreation program will provide a wide range of activities that promote fun, fitness, and cooperative participation in either a noncompetitive or friendly competitive atmosphere. For more information on CIRA Ontario, please visit www.ciraontario.com.